GOD'S
WISDOM
for a
MOTHER'S
HEART

A BIBLE STUDY FOR MOMS

BOBBIE WOLGEMUTH

THOMAS NELSON
Since 1798

NASHVILLE DALLAS MEXICO CITY RIO DE JANEIRO

Published in Nashville, Tennessee, by Thomas Nelson. Thomas Nelson is a trademark of Thomas Nelson, Inc.

Published in association with the literary agency of Wolgemuth & Associates, Inc.

The publisher is grateful to Lisa Guest for her writing skills and collaboration in developing the content for this book from the text of the *Mom's Bible*; notes written by Bobbie Wolgemuth.

Thomas Nelson, Inc., titles may be purchased in bulk for educational, business, fund-raising, or sales promotional use. For information, please e-mail SpecialMarkets@ThomasNelson.com.

Unless otherwise noted, Scripture quotations are taken from the New Century Version®. © 2005 Thomas Nelson, Inc. Used by permission. All rights reserved.

ISBN: 978-1-4185-4304-4

Printed in the United States of America

11 12 13 14 [QG] 5 4 3 2

CONTENTS

INTRODUCTION

Welcome to *God's Wisdom for a Mother's Heart: A Bible Study for Moms*. You're going to be a treasured part of the precious circle of moms who are on this parenting journey together.

It's scary but true . . . in order to drive a car, you and I had to pass both a written and a hands-on driving exam, but we didn't need to pass any test to become moms. The privilege of being a parent is total grace, a gift from God. Whether He blesses us with one or more children, naturally or through adoption, kids with unique qualities or special needs, He is entrusting each precious soul to our care.

And that perspective is very important: *our kids are not ours; they're God's.* He is trusting us to care for His handmade, one-of-a-kind creations. Best of all, that match—our kids and us—is not random. It's the Lord's plan that we each have the kids we have, and it's His plan that our kids have the mom they have. In light of the challenges of parenting, those pairings may seem puzzling at times. That's when we must choose to rest in God's divine sovereignty and perfect wisdom.

Thankfully, God speaks to us and shares that wisdom with us in His Word (please, please don't skip over the next section, "Why I Love God's Book"), and we can ask God to share His wisdom moment by moment, situation by situation, as we parent the sons and daughters He entrusts to us. After all, He will hold us accountable for our stewardship of each of them. Are we loving them well and growing them up to love Jesus? Are we passing the gospel truth on to our sons and daughters?

These people—the only ones on the planet who will ever call us "Mom"—change our lives. They bring sleeplessness but prayerfulness, noise and laughter, messes and memories, frustrations and joys. And along the way they teach us much about our heavenly Father's love for us—and we can trust that He will enable us to love them well.

Inside this study guide, you'll find some God-given guidelines and parenting principles for doing just that.

With my love and prayers for you to experience a joy-filled journey as a mom,

Bobbie Wolgemuth

5

WHY I LOVE GOD'S BOOK

In just the first four words of the Bible, we see one important reason why we need God's Book: "In the beginning God . . ." The Bible (God's Book) is all about God—the sovereign, eternal God—His creation, His plan for mankind, and His purpose for you and me and our families. His Book is a love letter from the Creator, who has had us in mind from the beginning of time.

Consider the Genesis account of Creation, where the phrase "then God said . . ." is repeated over and over. Each time God spoke, something came into existence; something marvelous, unique, and incredible happened. But the high point of Creation was when God said, "Let us make human beings in our image and likeness" (Genesis 1:26). You—and your children—not only have the fingerprints of Creator God all over you, but you are also made in His image.

As if creating us in His image were not amazing enough, God did something so astonishing that, in a quick read of Genesis 1 and 2, we could easily miss it. This time when God spoke, He spoke *directly to* the humans He had made: "God *blessed them and said* . . ." (Genesis 1:28, emphasis mine). The almighty God *talks* to humans. He loves us, He is interested in our families and our daily schedules, and He wants to talk to us—and we can actually understand His speech, His words, His ideas. That should be a compelling enough reason to read the Bible: it's the voice of God—creative, active, and alive, just as He is. But there's more. The Bible is the breath of God, the life-giving light from our Father, who wants to communicate with ordinary, frail moms like you and me—moms who need to know His transforming plan for our lives, fresh ideas for our homes, and how to best love our children.

Because of God's Book, we will not stumble around in this dark world. We will be able to fight back the voice that continually attacks the glorious truth of God's purposes. This vicious voice sows seeds of doubt about God's goodness by persistently asking, "Did God really say . . . ?" (Genesis 3:1). You and I have a clear choice: Will we make certain we know what God really said and then listen to His voice in His Word—or will we listen to His enemy's voice?

We who bear the image of God are privileged to have access to Him. We can hear Him speak as we read His Book. Through His Word, He provides us with wisdom for our parenting and courage to stand up for what is true and right. Therefore you and I, along with the children with whom God has blessed us, will be able to live lives that proclaim, "God is alive—and He is not silent."

God will amaze you as a direct result of the time you spend with Him reading and studying His Word. He's waiting for you right now.

HOW THIS STUDY WORKS

❧ *God's Wisdom for a Mother's Heart* is designed for your personal or group study and is based on the notes and insights in the *Mom's Bible*. You can use this study guide as a companion to the *Mom's Bible*, or it can be used with any Bible. If you already have a *Mom's Bible* or plan to get one, I've included the corresponding page number in the *Mom's Bible* for each Scripture reference. This will help you easily find the passage and give you more time to linger with the verses.

❧ Come to each study expectantly. God has some words of encouragement and guidance, hope and love, just for you, every time you open His Word. What will His message for you be today?

❧ Each lesson opens with a five-part "Mom Time" section for you to complete on your own, ideally one for each of the five mornings of your week. You'll be guided to both Old Testament and New Testament passages. You'll meet people—especially moms (some better role models than others)—from the Bible. And you'll think about how God's principles apply to parenting today.

❧ Next comes "Lean on Me: Learning from One Another." This portion is intended for you to work through with a small group, with whom you will meet once a week, because that's often how God teaches and encourages His people—through one another. And the moms in your small group may be especially helpful if, for instance, they have older kids than you do or if they got more sleep than you did the night before.

❧ "Bringing It Home" is a way to apply one idea from the week's study to life at home. Enjoy the time (it's homework you'll enjoy) with your kids that it encourages. The "Just for Fun" at the end of each lesson is a bonus opportunity for more fun!

❧ Closing each lesson is "Lean on Him: Learning to Trust God," an opportunity for group members to share prayer requests and to close their time together with a brief prayer.

❦ "Walking in Wisdom: Review and Remember" is a quick, five-point over-view of the week's lesson.

❦ One more word for you: grace! We know we need it as moms, and we know how to extend it to others. So come to the group meeting even if your pages from the week's lesson are a little low on answers.

A HANDFUL OF TIPS
FOR LEADERS AND PARTICIPANTS

* Pray for the women in your group and for the time you will spend together.

* Encourage women to attend the small group meeting even if they aren't able to finish their lesson during the week.

* Do your best to see that everyone has an opportunity to speak. Some of us have lots of say; others of us are, by nature, quiet in a group setting. If you're sitting across from a quieter woman, your eye contact and smile can encourage her to share.

* Remember that the pause between you reading the question and someone volunteering an answer may seem like a small eternity to you, but not to the group members. Keep in mind that many of these women are being careful to not monopolize the discussion; they probably have something to say, but they also want to give others an opportunity to share.

* Your task is to let God's Word do the speaking by centering on the questions "What is God saying in this verse?" and "What does it mean?"

* Before your circle breaks, talk about the "Bringing It Home" assignment for the coming week. Then, when you meet again, ask if anyone wants to share how her family was blessed or encouraged by the homework. Ideally, what a few of the moms share—smiling as they do so—will prompt some discussion about how to live out our faith at home.

* Protect the prayer time. Even though it is crucial to honor the commitment and end on time, don't let prayer reports, requests, or prayer time get pushed aside no matter how wonderfully the discussion is going. Prayer within your group, both together and throughout the week, will build faith as you see God at work in each of your lives.

❧ Every person in your group has her own needs, a unique personality, and different degrees of Bible knowledge. You will be wise to establish a few boundaries before you begin so time in your group is a safe and enjoyable experience for everyone.

- *Shhhhhh!* What is said in the group stays in the group. Because God's Word reveals the deepest intents of our hearts, often in a Bible study group, our emotions, confessions, feelings, and pain are brought out in the open. If the group hears information that is highly personal, it is important that every member honors the privacy pact. In fact, this important guideline is worth repeating: What is said in the group stays in the group.

- *Share the Time.* Because the Holy Spirit often speaks through the women in the circle with inspired ideas that will benefit others, encourage everyone to share during the time together. It helps to first point out the theme and then to ask often, "Who else would like to comment on that?" If the group moves away from the text, gently guide them back by saying, "We've wandered away from where we need to go. Even though this is interesting, can someone take us back to what this passage seems to be saying?" If someone tends to be quiet in the group, challenge her to speak up by saying, "Which one of the questions did you find especially helpful or enlightening?"

- *Share Your Heart.* Warm encouragement and participation help to create a warm circle. At the first group session, you may want to go around the circle and have each woman give her name, briefly describe her family, and then answer the question "Why did you come to this Bible study?" As you get to know one another more deeply, you will experience moments of bonding when your hearts are knit together— and you may experience tears. There will be times when you need to let someone cry, tell her story, share her pain, or weep openly. When this happens, be ready to embrace what the Holy Spirit is doing in your midst and say, "Your tears are a gift to us." It may be appropriate to stop the study and pray on the spot for a specific healing, pain, or situation.

It is best to invite the Lord to deal with the emotional component and pray His Word and His wisdom over the situation.

- *Show Up.* Be the cheerleader: "Even if you don't do your homework, come! God has a message just for you—and we still want to love on you." Moms have plenty of guilt without having it piled on because our homework isn't complete. Instead, let's be both encouragers and equippers to one another so every woman gets the most out of her Bible study. You have the ability to make others feel valued and stay connected in a safe place.

❧ Don't be surprised if the enemy makes it difficult for you to touch base with or pray for the women in your circle during the week. And it may sometimes seem as though everyone has a sick child or has a tough time getting out the door to Bible study. You are doing work that has eternal consequences, and Satan is not going to let it be easy for you or the others. One of the prayers for your group can be that no one would complete the study without a personal, saving knowledge of Jesus Christ. With that in mind, keep a sensitive heart and commit to pray for one another.

❧ Finally, as either a small group leader or participant, you have a special opportunity to pray for, encourage, and support the amazing women God places in your group. So consider any nervousness you experience as a place for God to step in and empower you. You do not have to have all the answers—because God's Word does! After all, when He calls—as He has called you—He equips. I know you will be blessed as you are a blessing to the women in your group.

1

FIRST THINGS FIRST: A MOM'S PRIORITIES

As moms, what kinds of different hats do we wear? How about . . . menu planner, cook, problem solver, chauffeur, personal shopper, tutor, referee, housekeeper, computer operator, washwoman, home-traffic controller, custodian, office manager, nurse, psychologist, pastor, chief executive officer, trash collector, playmate, fashion consultant, party planner, classroom volunteer, and often chief financial officer, dog whisperer, goldfish-flusher, coach, interior decorator, and gardener? And then some of us are even ambitious enough to take on church responsibilities and PTA positions—and we'd really like to work out more than once a month!

Research has shown that a typical mom logs more than ninety hours of work a week—and you're thinking, *A mom couldn't have done that research. It's definitely more than a hundred. I'm sure of it!*

With all this to do—and no one's arguing that this list is comprehensive—how do we know what to do first? Which things are of the *utmost* importance? God makes it clear in His Word.

MOM TIME

Here's what God wants moms to do:

1. LOVE HIM

⚜ As one pastor observed, it took Jesus Himself to distill the wisdom of Deuteronomy, a thirty-four-chapter book of rules for God's chosen people, Israel. According to Jesus' words in Matthew 22:37, 38 (page 1060), what is the most important commandment?

❧ On some days—in fact, perhaps during some minutes of every day—it may not seem as if you have much to offer God in the way of mind or strength, heart or soul. This is exactly how we can come to Him. In our emptiness, we are in a perfect position to receive all He wants to pour into us. In a typical mom day, what could it look like to love God with . . .

• all your heart?

• all your soul?

• all your mind?

• all your strength (Deuteronomy 6:5, page 199)?

❧ What key to loving God does Colossians 3:23 (page 1323) suggest? What hope and reassurance that you can obey God's greatest command do you find in this verse?

❧ What impact can loving God with all we are have on our perspective when we are doing laundry or cleaning toilets? When we are having a tough parenting day?

Inviting God into every moment of our day is a way to both love Him with all we are and rely on Him to work through us to raise our kids.

Lord, like every human being, I fall too far short of reaching my goal of really loving You. But I do love You, Father, and I'm grateful my experience of Your love for me does not depend on how faithfully and wholeheartedly I love You. Thank You for remembering that I am dust and for promising that nothing can separate me from Your love. Amen.

2. READ HIS WORD

❧ Turn to Psalm 119 (page 639) and read the following verses:

• Verse 11: What protection does the Bible give us?

• Verse 105: To what does the psalmist compare God's Word? Why are those two things important to you as a mom?

> WHAT DO I NEED TO KEEP IN MY LIFE, AND WHAT SHOULD I DELETE?

❧ Look also at Jesus' words in Matthew 4:4 (page 1029). Why do you think He compared Scripture to bread?

❧ According to 2 Timothy 3:16, 17 (page 1342), for what is God's inspired Word "useful" in terms of your calling as a mom?

❧ As you reacquaint yourself with Ruth (see page 284), you may see areas in her life that encourage your heart.

• What rather remarkable statement of faith did this Moabite woman make (Ruth 1:16, page 284)?

• What character qualities made Ruth the talk of the town (Ruth 2:11, 12, page 286)?

• In what wonderful ways did God bless Ruth for her faithfulness (Ruth 4:13, page 288)?

• What encouragement does God offer you in Ruth's story as you work diligently in the field of parenting?

God promises to use His Word to give us everything we need for living and serving Him (2 Peter 1:3, page 1383). God has blessed you with the kids who are filling your days, and He will sustain you through His Word. Have you set a goal to spend time with Jesus in His Word every day? What Bible reading plan might work for you during this season of your parenting? Do you believe God will give you some nugget from the Bible today that will be just the wisdom you need for today and tomorrow? He will honor and bless whatever time you spend in His Word.

Nurture your own faith with regular Bible reading—and yes, reading with your kids will nurture them, too . . . for sure! What they learn today is preparation for tomorrow, next week, future years . . . and for eternity.

Your Word, Lord, is the bread of life, it's the light to my path, and it's my instruction from Your Spirit. Yet I don't always make time to open my Bible and listen for what You want to say to me through a specific passage. Please make me hungry for Your Word, so hungry that I don't want to miss a day. Amen.

3. PRAY

❧ When should we pray?

- 1 Thessalonians 5:17 (page 1329)

❧ How should we pray?

- Philippians 4:6 (page 1314)

❧ Why should we pray?

- Psalm 34:4 (page 586)
- Psalm 145:18 (page 655)
- Luke 11:11–13 (page 1130)

❧ Who prays for us and with us—and why is this truth comforting?

- Romans 8:26 (page 1251)

❧ In Matthew 6:7–13 (pages 1032–33) Jesus offers us a model for prayer. Let's review the pattern of this model. What are the three ingredients of prayer in Jesus' example, and what is the important finish?

It's been said—and rightfully so—that the family that prays together, stays together.

What an amazing privilege You have provided for me, Lord Jesus. Because the blood of Christ allows me into Your presence, I can talk to You, the Creator and Sustainer of the universe, the Holy One, the awesome God, anytime I want . . . about anything I want. Teach me, Lord, to pray always, so I can enjoy this sweet communion with You. Amen.

4. LOVE YOUR NEIGHBOR

❧ What do these verses (on page 1391) teach about the kind of love God has for us and what He wants us to offer others?

- 1 John 3:16

- 1 John 3:17, 18

- 1 John 4:7, 10

❧ Now hear what God tells us about love through the apostle Paul. List the traits found in 1 Corinthians 13:4–7 (page 1276). Each one is a beautiful description of the love of Jesus that He shares freely with you. Put the names of your kids next to the quality of love each of them would most appreciate receiving this week. Focus on a simple way to share that kind of not-getting-upset, rejoicing-over-the-truth, trusting, or whichever-trait-you-chose love—and then ask the Lord to help you do it.

❧ Jesus often used a story to teach. Read Luke 10:25–37 (page 1129), the story of the good Samaritan. What warning does that story hold, especially for "task-driven" moms? If you're not sure, read "Walking in Attention" on page 1130 of *Mom's Bible*. What could you do to be a good Samaritan at home today? Be specific—and then courageously step out.

❧ What will your family do to love the neighbor next door, the widow down the street, or the homeless man who usually hangs out near the grocery store?

❧ What will members of your family do to love the orphan in Africa, people who lost homes in the latest hurricane or disaster, or the least-popular kid at school?

Remember: loving your neighbor starts with those very close neighbors—the people who share your address.

Lord, I can too easily relate to the men who walked right by the wounded man. Please open my eyes that I may see those in need—and unclench the fist with which I too often hold my day's agenda. Use me, please, as Your hands and feet in this world of needy, hurt people—especially those in the world of my home. Amen.

5. PRAISE AND THANK GOD

🌱 What reasons do you find in these verses to praise God and be thankful?

- Psalm 100:4, 5 (page 626)
- Psalm 139:14 (page 651)
- 1 Corinthians 15:55–57 (page 1280)

> I MUST FILL MY CUP VERTICALLY BEFORE I ATTEMPT TO GIVE TO OTHERS HORIZONTALLY.

🌱 Consider the relationship between humility and thanksgiving. If *humble* means "without resources," then why are humble people more likely to bow before God in praise and thanksgiving?

❧ In Hebrews 13:15 (page 1366) we are called to "through Jesus . . . always offer to God our sacrifice of praise." When can praise be a sacrifice? What is difficult for you to be thankful for? Think through what seems like a failure or problem and picture yourself lifting it up as an offering "through Jesus."

> Offer sacrifices of praise and thanksgiving—and receive from the Lord joy and hope.

Lord God, nothing changes my perspective on things like praise and thanksgiving. When I give you praise, it renews my hope and lifts my heart. Thank You for meeting me when I look to You with gratitude and amazement at Your immeasurable goodness to me. You are my Father and Friend, my Rock and Redeemer, my Everything! I praise You, Lord, and I thank You for making me Your child. Amen.

LEAN ON ME: LEARNING FROM ONE ANOTHER

❧ In your group, share one or two points from this week's study that were especially significant to you.

❧ What Scripture verse was especially meaningful when you came across it during your study? How did you experience instruction or encouragement from God's Spirit through those verses?

❧ Which priority is most firmly established in your life? Why do you think that is?

❧ Which priority is most difficult for you to keep at the forefront of your life? Why do you think that is? What practical ways do other moms in your circle make that priority happen in their lives?

❧ Think back over the past week. In what moments has God made His presence known to you? Those divine encounters may have happened as you were consciously living out these five priorities.

BRINGING IT HOME

What are you aiming for?

Every successful business or organization sets goals for itself and puts in writing where it is headed.

This week, write down your goals for yourself as a woman, a wife, and a mom. Include spiritual, personal, and family goals. Begin by asking the Lord, "What goals do You desire for me?" Also spend some time considering this three-part question:

When I die, what do I want to have accomplished as . . .

❧ a woman of God?

❧ a wife?

❧ a mom?

In all three areas, include attitudes, activities, and personal traits.

I was twenty-nine years old when I wrote my goals in a notebook, and those words have been a helpful touchstone in my life. I am so grateful for the wise Bible teacher who challenged me to both define the person I thought God wanted me to be and to move toward becoming that person.

Your goal setting will undoubtedly be a defining experience for you, and those goals will serve as tangible reminders of the priorities you want as the foundation for your life and your family.

You are more likely to reach goals if you take time to set them.

LEAN ON HIM: LEARNING TO TRUST GOD

Ask every mom in the group to request prayer for one thing for herself or her nuclear family. Go around the circle and ask, "How can we pray for you this week?" Take notes so you'll be able to pray for your group members throughout the week.

Close by having someone pray the following:

Lord God, thank You for clarifying what needs to take priority in my life—loving You with all I am, reading Your Word, praying, loving my neighbors, and giving You thanks and praise. Help me to approach these priorities with joy, not as merely items on my "to do" list, a set of tasks to perform and cross off. May I do these things because I love You. I remember that these priorities are the wellsprings of life abundant in You, with You, for You, and therefore for my children. In Jesus' name I pray. Amen.

WALKING IN WISDOM: REVIEW AND REMEMBER

Love God: Do all that you do as if you were doing it for Him, and you'll be loving Him throughout your day.

Read God's Word: Yes, it will make a big difference, even if you're reading a children's Bible with your kids!

Pray: Start each day with "Jesus, thank You for loving me with such incredible love. Today I want to be a woman who honors You. Please help me."

Love Your Neighbor: This starts with the "neighbors" under your own roof. Who needs an extra bit of mom love today?

Praise and Thank God: This perspective-changer will add joy to your heart and bring the fruit of God's Spirit into your home.

JUST FOR FUN

Here's a family project that kids of any age can enjoy. Write the words *PRAISE* and *THANKS* vertically on a piece of paper. Then, together as a family, list people or things you're thankful for that start with the letter *P.* Then move on to *R* . . . and *A* . . . you get the idea. When you're done, have someone read out loud this from-the-heart, homemade psalm.

2

PRAYING FOR OUR KIDS

What do your children need from you today? Definitely meals, probably some chauffeuring, maybe help with homework, perhaps some clothes washed . . . you know the specifics.

But what do your children need *most* from you today? Prayer.

Are you willing to spend as much time praying for your children as you do making their lunch or reviewing this week's spelling words?

Before you think this is just one more time-consuming thing to add to your "to do" list, let's look at creative ways moms can obey the command in Scripture to "pray continually" (1 Thessalonians 5:17, page 1329). Praying can be done anytime, in any place, and while your hands are busy with other things. It's the most important thing you can do for your children today and every day. It is a gift without equal.

Do you want to get serious about praying? Keep reading . . .

MOM TIME

1. A MOTHER'S PRAYERS

❧ We're pretty good at it. We've been doing it since we were about three years old. It's much easier to do than problem solving. And that "it" is whining. What was the Lord's reaction to the whining of His children in Numbers 11:1 (page 162)? What is the better option that Moses modeled in verse 2?

❧ Prayer is definitely a better choice than whining or complaining, but prayer is work—the most important work a parent can do. What commands or promises do you find in these verses?

- Psalm 34:4–7 (page 586)
- Proverbs 15:8 (page 675)
- James 5:16 (page 1374)

❧ What encouragement to pray do you find in the crying of a hurting parent found in Mark 9:23, 24 (page 1090)?

❧ What, if anything, keeps you from praying for your children as faithfully or as frequently as you'd like? What can you do to overcome those obstacles? Have you, for instance, considered your laundry room or the kitchen sink an altar for prayer?

❧ Tonight at dinner, share an amazing answer to prayer you have seen or received. Let your children join in on this conversation too. This reminder that God is mighty in the midst of praying people will encourage your kids to pray. It will also rekindle your own passion for prayer.

These verses on faith may strengthen your heart to want to be more diligent in seeking God in prayer: "Faith means being sure of the things we hope for and knowing that something is real even if we do not see it. . . . Without faith no one can please God. Anyone who comes to God must believe that he is real and that he rewards those who truly want to find him" (Hebrews 11:1, 6, page 1362). So when it comes to prayer, Mom, we're simply seeking God's heart.

Lord, I know it's important, and I know it's what You've told me to do. I also know it's the best gift of all for my kids. I know the enemy wants to distract me and keep me from praying. And I know my own sin nature interferes. But I do want to be a faithful seeker of God and a "prayer warrior" for each of my children. Please empower me to diligently focus on You and this very worthwhile, life-changing, transforming provision You've made—for the good of my children and for Your glory. Amen.

2. ADORATION AND CONFESSION

❧ Context is key, and the well-known A-C-T-S approach to prayer—*adoration, confession, thanksgiving,* and *supplication*—puts our prayers in the right context as we first approach God with words of adoration. What do you find to adore about God in these passages?

- Psalm 91:1, 2, 4 (page 622)

- Psalm 103:3–5 (page 628)

- Psalm 103:8–14

- 1 John 4:8–10 (page 1391)

❧ What value comes from adoring and praising God for who He is?

❧ Why does confession flow naturally after we spend time focused on and praising God?

❧ What words of confession does God's Word offer as examples for us?
- Psalm 51:1, 2 (page 598)
- Psalm 51:3, 4
- Psalm 51:10, 11
- Psalm 51:17 (page 599)
- Daniel 9:2–19 (pages 942–43)

❧ Do you believe in God's provision for you to live without regrets and to move on to fulfill your goal of abiding in Christ Jesus (see Philippians 3:12–14, page 1314)? What promises of forgiveness do you find in these passages?
- Psalm 51:7 (page 598)
- Psalm 103:12 (page 628)
- Isaiah 1:18 (page 720)
- Colossians 3:13 (page 1322)
- 1 John 1:8, 9 (page 1388)

When we come before God regularly to praise and adore Him, we see how holy and good He is. In light of His perfection, we can identify our sins and confess them.

Like Daniel, Lord, I want to pray with passion for the people I love, and I want to pray with passionate words of praise for who You are. And like David, I want to boldly and honestly confess my sins to You, my Redeemer and King. Please give me a tender and contrite heart, Lord, so I may move out of the past and run ahead into the new freedom You provide. Amen.

3. A MOTHER'S THANKFUL HEART

Let's spend some time with Hannah, a mom whose thankfulness has been immortalized in 1 Samuel 2:1–10 (pages 292–93).

• From this passage, list some reasons Hannah gave thanks to God. There are at least two reasons per verse.

• In these ten verses of thanks, how often does Hannah refer to her earlier request for a son? Comment on that.

• You may want to get to know Hannah a little better by reading her profile on page 293 in *Mom's Bible*. What about Hannah especially stands out to you? Why?

❧ What attribute of God's character would enable you to choose to be thankful even when circumstances are difficult?

❧ What practical value comes from giving thanks when we feel depleted, disappointed, or emotionally down?

❧ What expressions of thanksgiving for what God has done do you find in these verses?

- Psalm 100:4, 5 (page 626)
- Psalm 136:5–9, 23–25 (pages 649, 650)
- 1 Corinthians 15:56, 57 (page 1280)
- 2 Corinthians 9:10, 12–15 (page 1290)
- Hebrews 12:28, 29 (page 1365)

❧ In what current tough situation can you choose to find a reason—or maybe more than one—to be thankful? You can always linger on the truths of Lamentations 3:22, 23 (page 873), Luke 1:37 (page 1107), and Romans 8:29, 30 (page 1251).

Just as adoration fosters confession, thanksgiving fosters hope. Give thanks always (see 1 Thessalonians 5:18, page 1329) and watch God work in your heart as you wait for Him to work in every circumstance.

Like Hannah, Lord, I want to be a woman who not only prays but gives thanks—and not only when You answer prayers in the way and in the time frame that I want You to, but always. I want to be a woman who always thanks You for Your faithfulness, Your power, and Your love. I want the gift of faith to believe that You have a plan—even though I don't see it—and that You will accomplish what You desire in Your perfect time. Amen.

4. Sharing the Concerns of Our Hearts

Just as Hannah can teach us about thankfulness, a nameless New Testament mom can teach us another lesson—about prayer. Please turn to Mark 7:24–30 in *Mom's Bible* (page 1086), and read this woman's story.

• What was this mom's request?

• What everyday household scene did Jesus refer to when He first denied her request?

• What was the woman's quick response in verse 28? Explain her logic.

> God's Word is His voice. It is not always what I want to hear, but it's always what I need to hear.

❧ Now take a moment to read the brief commentary you'll find on page 1086 of *Mom's Bible* or look at Mark 7:25. What encouragement to pray do you find here?

❧ Take a look at another picture of persistent prayer—and, yes, there's some humor in it. In Luke 11:5–8 (pages 1129–30), which character represents God? Which character represents you and me? What lesson about prayer does Jesus teach in this story?

❧ In case someone didn't get the message, Jesus spoke very clearly in Luke 11:9–13. What did He emphasize in those verses? What about God's character inspires you?

❧ Maybe you don't know exactly what to pray for your children. Here are some verses to pray. Insert your child's name as you read and say them, turning them into a prayer. These verses are so rich; savor each one.

- Colossians 1:9, 10 (page 1317)
- Ephesians 3:16 (page 1304)
- Ephesians 3:17
- Ephesians 3:18
- Ephesians 3:19

Bold prayer, persistent prayer, specific prayer—we've seen encouraging examples of each of these today. We've also looked at ways we can pray for our kids. It will be a privilege to connect to God and our children as we pray specifically for their spiritual growth as well as the details of their lives.

Almighty God, thank You that prayer is not a matter of saying the right words the right number of times, but of coming from a heart that desperately seeks You. And thank You for inviting us to pray boldly, persistently, specifically about every detail of our lives. We want to want what You want, and we want to be in Your presence more than anything else. Amen.

5. Learning from a Man Named Job

❦ The most righteous man on earth, Job, had everything—and he lost it all. And, yes, that experience prompted complaints and spoken grievances, all of which fell away when God spoke in Job 38–41.

- The first three words of Job 38:4 (page 560) suggest the theme of these four chapters. What are those words, and what point is God making?

- From this passage or the notes on page 561 of *Mom's Bible*, what is striking about God's monologue before Job?

> ASK YOUR KIDS TO PRAY FOR YOU.

❧ What have you learned about God's character during those times of your life when you didn't understand or like what He was doing—or not doing?

❧ Read Isaiah 46:9–10 (page 774). Why is it good that we don't know all that will happen before it does?

❧ Read Isaiah 55:8 (page 784). Why is it good that God's ways aren't our ways? Recall a time when you prayed for something and you were sure it was what was best. Now, looking back, do you realize how shortsighted your request was, and are you glad that God did not give you what you had asked for?

❧ Read Mark 4:35–41 (page 1080), a New Testament postscript to this lesson on prayer.

• What was Jesus' reaction—or, perhaps more accurately, His nonreaction—as the waves crashed and wind howled?

• With this scripture or the insight on page 1081 of *Mom's Bible* in mind, what truth gives you comfort when your boat is being tossed around in a violent storm?

God promises to be with us always, and we can choose to believe, even when circumstances scream otherwise, as they did for Job and for the disciples on the boat during the storm, that God is still there. He always knows what's best.

As mothers, we will experience many times when we don't understand what God is doing. We can question God, pray, read our Bibles, and seek other counsel. But the best place to be is where Job found himself as God spoke to him in chapters 38–41: on our knees in repentance, recognizing that God is God, and we are not.

We too easily forget that our call to pray to God is an amazing privilege and gift. In the face of our overwhelming "to do" lists, we also easily forget that praying is one of the most important things we can do to serve our families. Can you commit to regularly praising the Lord for who He is, confessing your sins, thanking God for all that He has done for you and your family—and thinking of ways that He has blessed you? Pray specifically and expectantly about your concerns for your family.

Lord, when I face trials and when I am hurting and feeling deserted by You, I will choose to say in faith, like Habakkuk, "I will still be glad in the Lord; I will rejoice in God my Savior" (Habakkuk 3:18). Amen.

LEAN ON ME: LEARNING FROM ONE ANOTHER

❧ Share something new you learned about prayer from this week's study.

❧ What Scripture verse did you come across that was especially significant and meaningful during your study? What instruction or encouragement did you receive from God's Spirit in that verse?

❧ Praying is the most important thing we can do for our children today and every day. It is a gift without equal. So how can we daily incorporate praying for our children into the routine chores and events of our lives?

❧ What approaches to prayer have you found helpful? Do you use the A-C-T-S format? What other resources or guidelines for prayer have encouraged or enhanced your prayer life? Share those ideas with the group.

❧ Instead of just talking about prayer, pray. Spend some time praying through A-C-T-S, adoring God, confessing your sin (silently or out loud), thanking Him for the countless blessings He has given you, and sharing your supplications with Him, praying for specific people and situations. List your prayer concerns (a journal is a great place for this) and requests so you can incorporate them in the section for supplication.

BRINGING IT HOME

This week, choose an object—one for each family member—that will remind you to pray for your family. For instance, the hand lotion next to your sink can remind you to pray for the hands that will be practicing piano or swinging a baseball bat; your toothpaste tube can remind you to pray for your child who struggles with outbursts, that his words will be wholesome; a makeup mirror can remind you to pray for a child who needs to lighten up and smile more often; and your favorite coffee cup can remind you to linger a little longer with your husband before he goes out the door and to pray for him often during the day. In your mind, assign a specific member of your family to an object you use daily so you will remember to pray for that person every time you see and use it. These visible, personalized prayer reminders will remind you to lift each person to your heavenly Father's throne.

One more thing: sometime during the week, make a point of asking each person, "How can I pray for you today?"—and then do it.

LEAN ON HIM: LEARNING TO TRUST GOD

Ask every mom in the group to finish this sentence: "Because Jesus told me to pray about everything, one specific thing I would like to talk over with Him (after adoring Him, confessing to Him, and thanking Him) is . . ." As each one in the group tells about one thing she would lift up for herself or her family, take notes so you'll be able to join in praying for her throughout the week.

End the circle time together by having someone close with this prayer:

Loving Father, You have called to us to raise the children You have given us—to nurture them to know You, love You, and serve You. We confess that it is a bigger assignment than any of us can do on our own. Thank you for providing Your presence and the gift of prayer. We move forward

only by Your power and provision. O Father, create in our hearts a pas-
sion for prayer, for speaking to You and listening for Your voice Make
us, we ask, women who seek You first, so that we may become women of
faithful, persevering, expectant prayer. Amen.

WALKING IN WISDOM: REVIEW AND REMEMBER

A Mother's Prayers: Praying is not the only thing you can do; it is the most important thing you can do for your child.

Adoration and Confession: Adoring God means contemplating His holiness and His character and recognizing your sinfulness. When you confess your sins, He forgives, covers you with grace and mercy, and hears your prayers for yourself and others.

A Mother's Thankful Heart: "Give thanks to the Lord because he is good. His love continues forever" (Psalm 136:1).

Sharing the Concerns of Our Hearts: Be bold; be persistent; be specific as you pray for your children's spiritual growth as well as the details of their lives.

Learning from a Man Named Job: God's ways aren't our ways, and His actions—and sometimes inaction—can be puzzling. Humbled by this reality, we still trust in His presence with us and continue to pray to Him.

ꙥ JUST FOR FUN ꙥ

Go outside. Leave your iPod at home and your cell phone in your pocket. Just listen for what the Lord wants to say to you in the beauty and quietness of His creation. When you can, invite a child along. As you push the stroller or walk together, notice beauty in God's world. Offer a detailed color commentary on all the sights and sounds. "Isn't God amazing?" is all you'll need to say.

3

BEING OBEDIENT—AND TEACHING OBEDIENCE

When our kids were little, we regularly shared a little litany with them: "When do you obey Daddy and Mommy?" "The first time" was the right answer.

A friend of mine used a variation on the theme: "Obey—without discussion and without delay!"

These same guidelines for our kids work for God's kids, whatever our ages. We are to obey God without discussion and without delay. We are to obey Him the minute we know what it is He is telling us to do.

And as we obey God, we're showing our kids the importance of their obedience. So, if there is something you must do in obedience to God's Word, talk to your children about the choice you're making. Let them see that, although obedience is not always easy, it's always the right thing to do. Also, remember that requiring our kids to obey us, their earthly parents, is good training ground for learning to obey their heavenly Father.

Obedience is for all of us—and, as moms, we go first!

MOM TIME

1. THE SIGNIFICANCE OF OBEDIENCE

❧ What command do you read in John 14:15 (page 1181)?

❧ What promise in John 14:16 follows that command?

❧ What promise for our kids do you find in Ephesians 6:1–3 (page 1308)?

❧ What instruction for parents, specifically fathers, is spelled out in the second part of Ephesians 6:4? What does that look like in your home?

❧ According to Deuteronomy 28:1–8 (pages 218–19), what are some of the blessings that come with obeying God's commands? What does that mean today in your home?

Even though our culture doesn't applaud parental authority, as Christian parents, we are to lovingly provide structure for our children, and consistently require them to obey the rules we establish. Our efforts will be far more effective, however, if our kids see us submitting to God's authority in our own lives.

Lord, like Paul, "I do not do what I want to do, and I do the things I hate . . . I want to do the things that are good, but I do not do them. I do not do the good things I want to do, but I do the bad things I do not want to do" (Romans 7:15, 18, 19). I know Your commands are for my good. Thank You that, by the power of Your Holy Spirit, You can transform my heart—and the hearts of my kids—so that all of us can be more obedient to You. Amen.

2. Free Agents and Their Free Will

❧ They never tell you this at baby showers, but even as infants, our kids have wills of their own. We quickly see they are free agents and there are limits to the influence we have over them.

• What was the first indication of your firstborn's free will being strong and active?

• What's the most recent evidence that you've seen?

❧ Watching our kids function as free agents and sometimes ignore God's commands—and realizing that we sometimes do the very same thing—would be more frustrating were it not for the truth of the Spirit's work in us, described in 2 Corinthians 3:18 (page 1286). What hope for your parenting and for yourself do you find in this verse?

❧ One way we can reinforce and encourage obedience to God's ways is to praise and affirm our children when we see the fruit of the Spirit in their lives. Review Galatians 5:22, 23 (page 1299) and list the fruit of the Spirit below. Then look for an opportunity to affirm each of your children when he/she is exhibiting one of those traits. Make it your goal to do this by the end of the week—and when you do, point out to your children that their behavior suggests that they are walking in God's ways (i.e., obeying) and how that pleases the Lord (and you).

❧ While we're talking about affirming our kids, what command—and it is definitely applicable to parenting—do you find in Ephesians 4:29 (page 1305)?

❧ Now turn to Leviticus 26 (page 146). Verses 40–42 (page 147) set the scene.

• According to verse 43, why did God punish the children of Israel?

• Read verses 44, 45. What do these verses reveal about God's faithfulness and about why He chose to be faithful to Israel?

Leviticus sets forth rules and God's clear expectations for His people. Their (our!) disobedience resulted in serious consequences, yet He remained ready to extend forgiveness and grace. What can a mom learn about parenting from the way God dealt with the children of Israel here?

Make plain to your kids your expectations. Establish clear ground rules, and enforce them. Take seriously the responsibility of training and following through with your children. Always be ready to forgive them. Remember that you don't have the power to change your children's hearts or to make them decide to follow Christ and obey God's commands—and that is exactly why you pray for them. Only God changes hearts.

Lord God, as You well know from millennia of parenting experience, disobedient kids can be very, very frustrating. Please give me the energy to persevere in prayer and the training of my children, the strength to trust You to transform their hearts, and the readiness to tell them—no matter what they do or say—how much I love them. Amen.

3. HEARTFELT OBEDIENCE

❧ Tucked in toward the end of the commands of Deuteronomy 5 (pages 197–98) is a very tender and revealing statement by our heavenly Father. Read verse 29.

   • What twofold longing does the Lord reveal?

   • What twofold promise is implied?

   • What do you appreciate about the heart of God revealed here?

❧ Now let's consider our hearts, which are too often hardened against our gracious God.

   • What does God promise to do for us in Ezekiel 11:19 (page 885)?

   • According to Ezekiel 11:20, what will the positive consequences of His action be?

• Why is the condition of His people's hearts so important to God?

⁂ Turn back to Deuteronomy 4:29 (pages 196–97). The children of Israel were about to enter the promised land, and Moses chose this time to remind them that God's rules would still apply there. Life was still about following God, listening for His voice, knowing His commands, and walking obediently in His ways. As always—and as an example for us— God makes clear His expectations: He warns before He punishes. But, on a more positive note, according to Deuteronomy 4:29, what benefit or blessing is promised as a result of this kind of obedience?

⁂ Heart issues were very important in New Testament times, just as they are today. Skim Matthew 23 (pages 1061–62), slowing down to read verses 27, 28. Why was Jesus unhappy with the teachers of the law and the Pharisees He was addressing?

⁂ Now consider your heart.
  • In what ways, if any, are you like the hypocritical Matthew 23 teachers of the law and the Pharisees?

- In what ways, if any, is your heart hardened toward the Lord? If you're not sure, ask Him, and He'll show you.

 What do these verses tell you about the heart for God—the heart for obedience—that He desires His children to have?
  - Psalm 51:10 (page 598)
  - Psalm 51:17 (page 599)
  - Psalm 86:11 (page 619)
  - Proverbs 3:5 (page 661)
  - Ephesians 6:6b (page 1308)

Compliance is external; genuine obedience comes from the heart. In fact, living for God is a heart issue. Truly living for God means loving Him, respecting His ways, and obeying Him.

Lord, forgive me for the ways I go through the motions of obeying You. Help me acknowledge where I am dishonoring You, and then enable me to stop—especially since my kids are watching. My children do not have a perfect mother, but I want them to learn from me to come to You for a heart transformation. I know that this will require Your divine touch on my heart. I yield it to You. Amen.

---

4. FORGIVENESS WHEN WE SINFULLY DISOBEY

❧ Sometimes we disobey God and sin boldly, fully aware that we are doing the exact opposite of what God wants us to do.

- Read Jonah 2:7 (page 980). What is your impression of the man speaking these words?

- Now read Jonah 2:10. Notice in verse 7 that Jonah was inside the stinky belly of a fish, with slimy seaweed wrapped around him. When have you had to deal with the stinky, slimy consequences of willful disobedience?

❧ Sometimes we are blind to our own sin, and that was true for the apostle Paul—until his road-to-Damascus experience (Acts 9:1–8, page 1209).

- What sin was Paul confronted with? See verses 4 and 5.

❧ When, if ever, has someone, speaking God's truth in love, confronted you about the path you were walking or the sin you were much too comfortable with? What was the outcome of this conversation?

❧ If your kids had witnessed this interaction, what would they have learned from your example about how to deal with sin?

David, a man after God's heart and the handpicked leader of God's chosen nation Israel, was an adulterer, a murderer, and a liar. God confronted David about his sin through the prophet Nathan (2 Samuel 11, 12, pages 334–38), and David wrote Psalm 51 (pages 598–99) after that encounter. Read verses 1–17.

• What verses do you find especially striking? Why?

• Which verse or two could be your words right now for a sin you need to confess? What, if anything, is holding you back from asking God for forgiveness right now?

The bad news is that your sin and mine don't need to compare to David's to cause serious problems. But the corresponding good news is that no sin, no matter how vile, is beyond God's gracious forgiveness.

Holy God, we rank sin by degrees—but You don't. That's not easy for us to understand, but neither is the amazing truth that You graciously forgive any and every sin we confess. Thank You, because I know that, as I continue to learn obedience, I will still mess up and have much to confess. And when I repent, Your forgiveness is sure. Amen.

5. "EVEN IF . . ." OBEDIENCE

✽ Turn to 2 Kings 18:1–8 (pages 410–11) and meet Hezekiah, king of Israel eight generations after David.

• What did King Hezekiah do that pleased God but may not have pleased the people he was leading? See verse 4.

• What acts of obedience did Hezekiah pursue?

> REPENTING IS
> TELLING CHRIST
> EXACTLY WHY
> YOU NEED HIM.

• What evidence of God's blessing on Hezekiah do you see?

✽ Remember King Nebuchadnezzar and the fiery furnace into which he threw Shadrach, Meshach, and Abednego? The story is in Daniel 3 (pages 932–34).

• What command of the king had these young Hebrew men chosen to ignore?

• What command did they choose to obey? From whom?

• What is striking about their words to Nebuchadnezzar? See verses 16–18.

• What do their words suggest about what was and was *not* motivating their obedience?

• What is motivating your obedience to God?

❧ In Luke 1, we read about Elizabeth and learn that she had been unable to have a child in an era when the inability to conceive not only impacted family lines but also suggested God's disfavor. Her situation was heart-breaking and humiliating.

• What do you learn about Elizabeth and her husband, Zechariah, in verse 6 (page 1105)?

• What impact did Elizabeth's childlessness have or not have on her devotion to the Lord and her way of life?

• What message did the angel Gabriel have for Zechariah and Elizabeth? See verses 13–17.

> WHAT WILL MY KIDS STRUGGLE WITH IN TWENTY YEARS BECAUSE I REFUSE TO DEAL WITH THIS SIN OR BAD HABIT NOW?

• What does Elizabeth's example teach us about obedience?

❧ Despite her disappointment and heartache, Elizabeth did not turn away from God. She continued to obey Him, undoubtedly finding peace in His proven trustworthiness even as she trusted in His faithfulness. For what are you waiting on God? Has the wait impacted your commitment to Him, your willingness to obey, and/or your attitude toward Him or toward life? Why not? Or if it has, what will you do to release the bitterness and disappointment and reconnect with God and the hope He offers?

❧ What words of hope and trust do you find in Psalm 27:13, 14 (page 582)? What impact can that hope have on your obedience to God?

❧ Now turn to Psalm 112:1 (page 636). Why is that an appropriate closing for our lesson on obedience?

Psalm 112:1 and the promises found in the verses that follow are a great encouragement to obey the Lord's commands. We read that our children will be powerful, that each generation will be truly happy, and that—in God's economy—they will be wealthy. There are some great rewards for us as well: light in the darkness (a reward for honesty, kindness, mercy, goodness, and generosity), victory (in return for fairness), a steady heart, security, confidence, and great honor. Obedience may not be an easy path, but it's the right path.

It's plain and simple. Disobedience brings undesirable consequences and trouble. Obedience brings blessing. It seems like a clear choice, doesn't it? Obedience is the obvious and easy choice to make, yet we need God's strength to make it.

Your Word clearly sets forth Your commands, Lord. I do want to obey You—and I want my obedience to be heartfelt and motivated by my love for You. May my obedience also teach my kids the importance of their obedience to You as well as to their parents. Empower my children and me, Lord, to obey all that You command, and to do so joyfully. Amen.

LEAN ON ME: LEARNING FROM ONE ANOTHER

⁂ Share one or two points from this week's study that were especially significant to you.

⁂ What Scripture verse was especially meaningful when you came across it during your study? What instruction or encouragement did you receive from God's Spirit as you read that verse?

⁂ Obedience brings many blessings, so why don't we obey? Share some of the reasons you struggle—and learn from one another how to choose obedience over disobedience.

⁂ Which real-life picture of obedience (Hezekiah, Elizabeth, Shadrach, Meshach, and Abednego) or disobedience (Jonah, David) found in this lesson did you find especially helpful? Why did you choose that example?

❧ What blessings of obedience to God have you experienced in your life?

BRINGING IT HOME

Sometimes a problem is just too big for us—or our kids—to handle, and we can't stop thinking about it. When we follow the God who commands, "Do not worry about anything" (Philippians 4:6), we are disobeying Him if we keep holding on mentally and emotionally to that situation. So here is an idea to try this week—and it works well with younger people too.

Place an empty gift box on the counter or dining room table, and when a certain set of circumstances is too hard for you to deal with, and you are consumed with fret or worry, open the box. Picture yourself placing those circumstances inside as a "gift" for God, and close the lid. Then turn away, knowing that the situation is in His very capable hands and very wise care. When I do this with my "blue box" I say to the Lord, "I now choose to focus my thoughts on You. Will You keep me from dwelling on things I can't control?" That closed box reminds me that I can think about the circumstances later, but in the meantime I'm not worrying—and I *am* obeying:

"Give all your worries to him, because he cares about you." (1 Peter 5:7)

Young children may want to decorate their own boxes to keep in their bedrooms, and when they are having trouble dealing with anger or disappointment, they can open the boxes and put all their frustrations inside.

LEAN ON HIM: LEARNING TO TRUST GOD

Ask every mom to pray about one thing for herself or her nuclear family. Take notes so you'll be able to pray for your group members throughout the week.

Close by having someone pray the following:

It's not always easy to do what's right. It's not easy for us or for our kids. But, Lord, Your commands are for Your glory and for our good. Please kindle a passion to obey You in our hearts and in the hearts of our children, a passion rooted in our love for You. Amen.

WALKING IN WISDOM: REVIEW AND REMEMBER

The Significance of Obedience: We show our love for Jesus when we obey God's commands, and then His blessings follow. We won't effectively teach obedience to our kids, though, if we aren't submitting to and obeying the Lord's commands.

Free Agents and Their Free Will: Clear ground rules, intentional training in God's ways, ready forgiveness, prayer for the Holy Spirit to work in their hearts—these are key dimensions of a Christian parent's job.

Heartfelt Obedience: We need to repent of any hardheartedness and hypocrisy. Then, because of God's gracious work in us, we can respond to His commands with heartfelt obedience.

Forgiveness When We Sinfully Disobey: We will mess up—intentionally as well as unintentionally—even as we strive to obey God. Thankfully, no sin we commit will be beyond His gracious ability to forgive.

"Even If . . ." Obedience: We are to obey God out of our love for Him and whether or not He answers our prayers the way we want Him to or when we want Him to. He can enable us to do so—and to do so with joy.

❧ JUST FOR FUN ❧

Surprise your children with an invitation to whip up a batch of homemade chocolate chip cookies. Yes, from scratch. Enjoy your kids and the mess! And when you're enjoying this homemade treat (with milk), talk about the importance of following the recipe . . . and about the truth that obeying God in life is a lot like following a recipe in the kitchen. Good things happen when we do exactly what the recipe—and God's Word—says.

4

DISCIPLINE:
DO THE RIGHT THING

Okay, be honest. What comes to mind when you hear the word *discipline*? Do you think of punishment? Dieting? Grueling preparation for a marathon? The word "no"? How about anger or power or denial?

Discipline is the ability to do the right thing at the right time for the right reason. It often does involve saying no—God says "no" to us; we say "no" to our children and ourselves—in order to say yes to something better. Keep that definition in mind as you consider this week's discussion of discipline. Whether we're talking about God's discipline, a parent's discipline, or self-discipline, it really is a very *good* thing. Our key verse is Hebrews 12:11 (page 1364).

MOM TIME

1. THE "D" WORD

🎜 *Discipline* comes from the Latin *disciplina*, meaning "teaching and learning." And that's what discipline is really all about: teaching and learning. An experiment that took place on a school playground illustrates the positive role that discipline can play in our lives. When the playground was fenced along the perimeter, the kids played freely throughout the fields, the blacktop, and the track. When the fence was removed, the kids huddled together in the center.

  • Why do you think the kids gravitated toward the center of the play area when the fence was gone?

- What does this experiment suggest about rules—their role, their importance, and their impact?

- When have you felt more secure: once you learned the rules or felt the boundaries?

❧ When have you seen your children more peaceful once you've talked with them about what behavior was appropriate and what wasn't?

❧ We need to know what's right so we can feel safe. Because we all have sinful natures, we'll want to push those limits, but consider some positive dimensions of those limits:
  - Proverbs 3:11, 12 (page 661)
  - Proverbs 29:17 (page 691)

❧ We can experience God's discipline when He allows the consequences of our sin to play out. According to Psalm 66:10 (page 605), what is another way we can experience God's discipline? What does this metaphor mean?

❧ What are your goals in disciplining your children? List at least one for each category.

- Spiritual

- Emotional

- Relational

- Mental

- Physical

❧ You undoubtedly have goals for yourself as well, and reaching those will require self-discipline. What are some of those goals? List at least one for each category.

- Spiritual

- Emotional

- Relational

- Mental

- Physical

> BUILD A HOME
> WHERE PEOPLE
> ARE TREATED
> WITH HONOR
> AND LOVE,
> WHERE
> DISCIPLINE IS
> CONSISTENT,
> AND WHERE
> GRACE IS
> ABUNDANT.

Discipline—God's, a parent's, and self-discipline—are all about teaching and learning. As moms, we're doing the teaching kind of discipline for our children even as we learn from the Lord as He disciplines us.

Lord God, when I'm disciplining my kids, help me to be firm and compassionate. Help me to remember that I'm not especially fond of Your discipline, neither the strengthening-of-my-faith kind of discipline nor the consequences-of-my-sins kind. Please keep me tender, I pray, even as I ask You to give me wisdom and strength to persevere in this important requirement of good parenting. Amen.

2. GOD'S DISCIPLINE

❧ Discipline and love go hand in hand. God, the perfect Parent, always gives clear instructions, He warns before He punishes, and He always acts for our good and His glory. Read Revelation 3:19 (page 1404).

   • According to the first part, why does God discipline us?

   • According to the second part, what is the purpose of God's discipline?

❧ Sometimes our heavenly Father finds it necessary to discipline us, His children.

   • Read Hebrews 12:7–11 (pages 1363–64) and note the good that comes from God's discipline.

• Jeremiah 30:11 (page 836) makes an important statement about God's discipline. What does He say?

❧ Sometimes God allows testing not as a consequence of our unacceptable actions—our sin—but to accomplish something else in us. What do these verses say about His goal for that kind of discipline?

• Psalm 66:10 (page 605)

• James 1:2, 3 (page 1367)

• 1 Peter 1:6, 7 (page 1375)

❧ One form of God's discipline that both moms and kids can experience is the discipline of waiting.

• What lessons have you learned as you've waited for God to answer your prayers?

• What words of encouragement can you give to your kids as they wait for God to answer their prayers?

❧ What circumstance are you and/or your kids praying about and waiting for God to answer right now? Be sure to take this opportunity to talk with them about God's perfect wisdom, His perfect love, His perfect timing, His big-picture perspective on our lives, and how well He knows us and therefore knows what is good for us.

❧ God disciplines us because He loves us, and there is a self-discipline we can embrace that tells Him that we love Him. It is the discipline of remembering. We read in Deuteronomy an account of Moses leading the children of Israel in this kind of exercise.

• Read Deuteronomy 2:7 (page 193). What had God done for Israel?

• Read Deuteronomy 1:29–33 (page 192) and note some specific examples of God's blessing and protection.

• Now list some specific examples of God's blessing and protection in your life, in the good times as well as the wilderness times. Then let the kids share some of their own memories.

With your children, pay attention each day to the many ways, big and small, that God has faithfully led and provided for your family. This discipline of remembering His faithfulness will prove to be a firm place to stand when the future feels shaky, when you're being disciplined by your heavenly Father, or when you're waiting for Him to answer your prayers.

Lord, sometimes Your discipline doesn't feel like love, but it's necessary. Please keep me sensitive to that fact when I discipline my kids—and please enable me to do what's best for them even if they don't like it—or me—in the moment. I also ask that You use the times when we are all waiting on You—and on answers to our prayers—to grow our faith in You. And thank You that our family can have fun with the discipline of remembering Your past goodness today. Amen.

3. SELF-DISCIPLINE

❧ **Quiet Solitude:** Have you noticed how we're surrounded by so many noisy distractions? And sometimes it feels like the noise is louder for moms as we juggle full schedules and tackle never-ending "to do" lists. What we need is quiet. And solitude. Jesus knew He needed quiet time alone with God in order to listen and to do what God had called Him to do. You and I need quiet solitude, too (Mark 1:35, page 1074).

- What command do you find in Psalm 46:10 (page 595)? (And it is a command, not a suggestion!)

- What promise do you find in Isaiah 30:15 (page 751)?

- What example of making time to be quiet do you find in Psalm 131 (page 647)? Notice who the (busy) author of this psalm is. Being a king was a big job.

- Is time for solitude—time to be alone with Jesus—a regular part of your schedule? If so, what do you do to protect it? If not, what can you do to overcome whatever is standing in your way?

- If you regularly spend time alone with Jesus, what are some of the blessings and joys that come from your time with Him? Talk to your kids about these sweet times with the Lord, and encourage them to learn to listen to what Jesus has to say to them.

❦ **Saying No:** Sometimes busy moms become busier moms because they forget to use the word "no".

- What was the most recent time that you said "yes" when you really wanted to say "no" or realized later you should have said "no"? Why did "yes" come out of your mouth?

- What can you do to avoid over-scheduling when you need to say "no"?

❧ Now that you've given it some thought, let me offer a couple of tips: When you're asked to do something don't say "yes" right away—but buy yourself some time with "I'll get back to you," "I'd like to pray about that," or "I need to talk to my husband/check my calendar." That way you'll have time to ask the Lord for wisdom and think about it before blurting out a quick "yes" that you'll regret later. Also remember: you don't need to give a reason. A simple "no, that just won't work out" or "no, that's not a good time for our schedule" will suffice.

It's important to strengthen your "no muscle"—and it's important for your kids to strengthen theirs, too! The ability to say "no" is not just for major or bad or dangerous things, but for everyday decisions we make. You and your kids can start practicing by saying "no" to having that extra dessert, staying in bed after the alarm goes off, or playing a computer game instead of reviewing for the next day's exam. Make a point to occasionally ask at the dinner table, "What did you say 'no' to today?" One night this week, lay the foundation for this family game by talking to your kids about how important it is to make a promise to ourselves—and then to keep it. Journal here about your experience.

❧ **Doing What Needs to Be Done:** "But I don't feel like doing it, Mom!" Ever heard that before? (What mom hasn't?) But if we only did things we *felt* like doing, a lot would be left undone! It's self-discipline, not unrestrained enthusiasm, that gets us doing the day's third load of laundry, changing the day's twelfth diaper, or getting in the car for the eighth time ... in one day. A servant's heart can help fuel this kind of self-discipline. What does God's Word teach in these passages?

- Matthew 25:40 (page 1065)
- John 13:14, 15 (page 1180)
- Galatians 5:13, 14 (page 1299)
- Colossians 3:17 (page 1322)

❧ Daniel offers us a good example of self-discipline, specifically, premeditated self-discipline. Read Daniel 1 (pages 929–30).

- What were some of the perks of being taken into Nebuchadnezzar's palace? See verse 5 in particular.

- According to verse 8, what did Daniel decide?

- In what ways can we prepare our children for the choices or temptations they will face? And what can we do to help them decide, as Daniel did (and figuratively speaking), what not to eat, *before* they're hungry?

❧ In sharp contrast to Daniel, we see a lack of self-discipline in Eve. But before any of us casts the first stone, let's consider what may have been behind that deficit. Read Eve's portrait on page 6 of *Mom's Bible* or Genesis 3:1–6 (pages 4–5). Look closely at the serpent's words: "Did God *really* say . . . ?" The serpent was sowing seeds of doubt about God's character, integrity, and faithfulness. What picture of God did the serpent paint?

• Eve was unable to trust God. She didn't believe that God loved her enough to plant a "no" right in the middle of this amazing garden for her own good. Eve was afraid that God wouldn't come through for her. What fear—ongoing or brand-new—are you dealing with today? What concerns (read "fears") for your children are preoccupying you? What can you choose to believe about God?

• Daniel was a good example, and Eve serves as our "what not to do" example. And what about us? When do we fear that God won't come through?

> OCCASIONALLY, WHEN THE NEED TO DISCIPLINE ARISES, ASK YOUR CHILD, "IF YOU WERE THE MOM, WHAT WOULD YOU DO?"

We have the ability to choose to steady our minds by focusing on this basic thought: "God is great, and God is good." Young children say it at the breakfast table, and it is true. Even when we do not understand God's ways, we ask for the gift of faith and can decide to trust and obey Him.

Lord, help me to follow in Jesus' footsteps and make time to be with You. I also ask You to help me—and to help me help my kids—decide what we're "going to eat and not going to eat"—before we're hungry. When I'm overwhelmed with fear and tempted to mistrust You, remind me of Your incredible love and faithfulness. You are great, and You are good . . . all the time. I will trust and obey what I know from Your Word to be true about You. Amen.

4. DISCIPLINE IN THE HOME

Discipline is definitely one of the most difficult and relentless challenges of parenting. In the short term, a parent's failure to discipline may keep "peace" in the home, but what are possible long-term consequences of failing to discipline our children? And what are possible long-term blessings of consistently disciplining them? The following verses address both.

- Proverbs 13:24 (page 673)
- Proverbs 19:18 (page 680)
- Proverbs 22:6 (page 682)
- Proverbs 23:13, 14 (page 684)
- Proverbs 29:15 (page 691)

❧ A passive father to his sons, the Old Testament prophet Eli serves as a negative example of parenting.

• What do we learn about Eli's sons in 1 Samuel 2:12 (page 293)?

• What example of their evil is outlined in verses 13–16?

• According to verse 17, what was God's opinion of Eli's boys?

• Turn to 1 Samuel 4:14–18 (page 296). What tragic end did Eli's family meet?

❧ Instead of just pleading with your children to obey, look for ways to follow God's example in your home: God has always taught His people through the natural or logical consequences of their actions. It's important, however, to react calmly and not let yourself get in an emotionally charged struggle. For instance, you can gently say, "I'm sorry you are upset about your earlier bedtime. You remember that this is the consequence you chose when you stayed in bed this morning after I woke you up."

• Read Judges 2:10–18 (page 258). These verses reflect Israel's pattern (and ours). What were the logical, albeit supernaturally allowed, consequences of Israel's disobedience?

• What opportunities do you have to enforce logical or natural consequences in your home? Maybe your teenage daughter is having trouble

73

speaking respectfully to you. Would it be logical—and painful for her—to take away her cell phone for a while? Be prayerful as you establish consequences, and take courage in God's power as you enforce them.

❧ Kids seem to have extra sensitive radar for what is not fair in their world. If a sibling is being treated differently, brother and sisters will not be shy about saying, "Hey, that's not fair!" Or if our punishment is administered by us in selfishness or uncontrolled anger, they will quickly pick up on the attitude and can totally miss the point of the discipline. Kids do have a way of bringing out the ugly stuff inside our own hearts, don't they? They often are the very tool God uses to refine us and deal with attitudes that never surfaced before we had children. We are not perfect moms, but we know where to go for help. We can ask the Lord for wisdom and self-control when our children need our calm and effective discipline.

• Read Leviticus 24:19–21 (pages 143–44). What about the punishment or consequence spelled out here is fair? How does the consequence match the infraction?

• What childhood experience of being disciplined sticks with you as being unfair or administered out of anger? What does your perspective now suggest about the situation? How can you avoid repeating a harmful pattern modeled in your childhood? With the Holy Spirit's help, you can be a cycle breaker. Romans 8:25, 26 (page 1251) will give you courage to believe it.

• What very appropriate and fair consequence made a helpful impression on you when you were growing up? What biblical principles for discipline can you now begin to apply in your own home?

Nurturing our children's spiritual lives takes diligence, initiative, and time. There is no substitute for a parent's role in their lives. Our kids need spiritual strength to face the evil in our culture. Consciously make teaching and training them in righteousness your highest priority.

I am so thankful, Lord, that when You call me to do something, You empower me. I do need Your help, Your guidance, and Your strength if I am to parent in a godly manner and effectively discipline my children. Amen.

5. The Discipline of Gratitude

Today we're going to talk about a more tangible kind of self-discipline as we consider who owns all we have. Look at 1 Chronicles 29:17 (page 453) and notice what pleases God. What is said here about the heart and attitudes?

❧ According to Leviticus 27:30 (page 149), what is required of God's people? Why?

❧ To help your kids understand who owns all that your family has, you may use a simple illustration to teach them about stewardship. Hold ten dimes in your hand. Explain that all we have comes from God's bountiful supply. Take one dime from your hand and tell the children that we show our gratitude to God by joyfully giving a portion back to Him. The second dime represents the portion that goes into savings. Now show your kids what is left in your hand and say, "This is the part our family uses for our needs. God supplied the ten dimes in the first place, and He wants us to trust Him to supply our needs at all times." Philippians 4:19 (page 1316) is a great verse to have them write down and talk about.

❧ We honor God when we put everything—our time and our talents as well as our treasures—before Him for His kingdom use. As you look into this mirror of Scripture, what is God saying to you about your attitude and your giving?

❧ As your kids watch you, what talents do they see you joyfully sharing with God and His people? What time? And what treasures?

God is waiting to show us how powerful and able He is to meet our physical needs and sustain us to serve others. When we discipline our hearts to trust and obey Him, we can move beyond fear and selfishness and experience His power to be cheerful givers.

Why does Christ correct and punish and discipline His family? He loves us too much to leave us alone in our sin, fear, selfishness, and rebellion. Likewise, we show our children our love for them by consistent training and correction. Keep in mind your child's future, and remember what Hebrews 12:11 says: "We do not enjoy being disciplined. It is painful, but later, after we have learned from it, we have peace, because we start living in the right way." Our most important task is to prepare our children for the life of peace and fruitfulness God intends for them.

Lord, thank You for the generous talents, abilities, and possessions You have entrusted to me. Thank You for the privilege of giving back to You anything You choose to use for Your kingdom work. Please help my children cultivate grateful hearts and experience the joy of this discipline called stewardship. I want them to see both how important it is to honor You and how faithful You are. Amen.

LEAN ON ME: LEARNING FROM ONE ANOTHER

❧ Share one or two things from this week's study that were new or significant to you.

❧ What Scripture verse was especially meaningful when you came across it during your study? What instruction or encouragement did you receive from God's Spirit as you read that verse?

❧ At the beginning of this lesson, you noted some specific goals you have for your children. Share with the group some methods and ideas that you have found especially effective in your efforts to guide your kids toward spiritual, emotional, relational, mental, and physical discipline.

❧ Now talk together about effective methods of discipline—specifically, the use of logical or natural consequences—that you've used in your home. Also take some time to share what you do to maintain an appropriate attitude and stay strong during the enforcement stage.

❧ Talk together about how your family is being intentional about serving with the time, the talents, and the treasures God has given you. Get ideas from other members of the group. Listen for ways that both generations can incorporate generous giving and an attitude that will please the Lord in your home.

BRINGING IT HOME

With its ruffled edge, it was definitely a unique spoon, and that made it perfect for the unique role it played in our family. Every once in a while, that spoon would appear next to someone's dinner plate as a cue to talk about something special that person had done or said. The "special spoon" gave our family the opportunity to honor one person by celebrating a kind word spoken to a sibling, a helping hand offered to a neighbor, a noble attitude, or a humble (and until then) quiet act of service. Even though it was just a spoon, it became a much-desired trophy.

As moms, we are always on the lookout for a moment when we can encourage and affirm our children. This week have your own dinnertime reward ceremony. Keep your eyes open for a praiseworthy word or deed, and honor the person who was "caught" in the kindness.

Your special spoon (or cup or plate or whatever you choose) will encourage everyone to keep their eyes open for random acts of kindness.

LEAN ON HIM: LEARNING TO TRUST GOD

Ask every mom in the group to request prayer about one thing for herself or her nuclear family. Take notes so you'll be able to pray for your group members throughout the week.

Close by having someone pray the following:

Father in heaven, You love us perfectly. You discipline us, Your children, and we thank You for loving us enough to correct us. Help us to be open to learning whatever You want us to learn from the consequences of our sin, as well as from the fires You allow to purify our faith. Fill us with Your Spirit so we can be self-disciplined in ways that honor You and are

healthy for us. And, finally, give us creativity, wisdom, and energy as we discipline the children You've entrusted to our care. Amen.

WALKING IN WISDOM: REVIEW AND REMEMBER

The "D" Word: God's discipline of us, our discipline of our children, and self-discipline—we are always both teaching and learning.

God's Discipline: God disciplines us because He loves us, just as we discipline our children because we love them. Trusting His love and remembering His faithfulness will sustain us in those times when we wait for God to work.

Self-Discipline: Time with the Lord is the key to other aspects of self-discipline, to knowing when to say no, to doing what needs to be done, and to serving others with the right motivation.

Discipline in the Home: Active involvement, the use of logical and natural consequences, consistent enforcement of those consequences, and fairness—disciplining our children is daily, relentless, and absolutely crucial.

The Discipline of Gratitude: All you have is the Lord's—your time, talents, treasures, and kids—and you are to honor Him as you take care of every one of these good gifts from your heavenly Father's hands.

JUST FOR FUN

Today we can send greeting cards that have a computer chip that speaks on its own or records our voice. We can send e-mail greeting cards and texts to say, "i luv u." This week try a simple and wonderful way to say, "I love you." Here it is . . . smile every day. Yes, that's it. Be intentional about looking into each family member's eyes at some point in the day, smiling, and saying, "I love you!" Then enjoy what happens in your home. Wouldn't it be wonderful to see that smiles are as contagious as yawns? ☺

GROWING CHRISTLIKE CHARACTER

It's a much-loved New Testament verse that many a believer can quote verbatim: "We know that in everything God works for the good of those who love him" (Romans 8:28).

In the next verse we read what that "good" involves: "God chose [those who love him] to be like his Son" (verse 29). Becoming more like Christ—that's God's purpose as He works in our own lives, and He uses us as moms to help our children grow to please Him and display the character of Jesus in their lives.

MOM TIME

1. Choose to Love . . . Selflessly

❧ When you think about selfless love, what biblical image or event comes to mind? The picture in 1 John 4:10, 11 (page 1391) is my first thought.

❧ Read 1 John 3:16–18 (page 1391). What guidelines for loving others does God give believers in this passage?

❧ In what way(s) have your observed Jesus-followers investing their lives for others? Be specific. And in what ways are you loving people "not only with words and talk, but by [your] actions and true caring" (verse 18)?

❧ Which of these activities—which dimensions of life-giving love-in-action—are your kids aware of? What do or could you say to help them learn that helping people is one way we show those people Jesus' love? Share with them the story Jesus told in Matthew 25:31–46 (pages 1065–66).

❧ Showing people in our family Jesus' love is a beautiful way to "give our lives for others." Doing a sibling's chore, helping Mom or Dad without being asked, offering to read to a young or elderly person—family members of all ages can get involved with love-in-action. What can you do together as a family to show people Jesus' love? Here's a jump start for your brainstorming session. When you're done, put a couple of these on your calendar and commit to follow through.

• Invite a neighbor child in for cookies, hugs, and a story

• Take a meal to a family

• Wash the elderly neighbors' car or mow their lawn

• Work together in a Sunday school class for little kids

Talk is easy. Love-in-action takes effort. It's what God commands—and that's clearly how He showed His love. Jesus didn't just talk about His love for us; He died on the cross to make sure we understand.

Lord, as I walk through my days, please keep me sensitive to any opportunities to put love into action—both inside and outside my home. It's too easy to get wrapped up in what I need to do. I don't want to miss out on the chance to love someone with Your love. Amen.

2. CHOOSE TO SERVE . . . JOYFULLY

❧ Read Luke 22:24 (page 1149). "Them" is Jesus' disciples—what concern are they addressing in this verse? What attitude does their arguing suggest?

❧ Our society idolizes the wealthy, powerful, beautiful, athletic, and even the brazenly immoral. What radically different standard for greatness did Jesus identify in Luke 22:25–27?

❧ Clearly, the call to be a servant dovetails with the command to love with our actions, not just with our words. And the attitude of our hearts is key to both. Based on each verse below, what attitude pleases God?

- Proverbs 15:33 (page 676)
- Philippians 2:3 (page 1312)
- Titus 3:2 (page 1346)
- 1 Peter 5:5 (page 1382)

❧ When have you experienced heartfelt joy in serving? Those satisfying moments are gifts that come as we do what God created us to do—serve as Jesus did.

❧ What keeps us from serving? What keeps us from serving with joy? What can we do to overcome the selfish attitude or the details of everyday life that interfere with our loving and serving?

Jesus calls us to serve selflessly in a "me-first" world, to love without complaint, and to seek no recognition for ourselves. Be alert to opportunities for your family to serve so that your children can practice putting others first. Let them experience the joy of servant greatness.

Lord God, sensitize me to opportunities to serve, empower me with Your love and joy, and remind me to pray for those I serve, in obedience to Your commands and for Your glory—and Your glory alone. Amen.

3. Choose to Stay Faithful . . . Confidently

❧ Waiting is something few of us would volunteer for, yet often a season of waiting is a good gift from God. Oh, not always good in the moment, but always in the long run. What has God allowed you to wait for in your life? As you look back, what benefits and blessings do you see as the fruit of that time?

❧ You and I aren't the only ones who have struggled with waiting on God. Consider King Saul. Read 1 Samuel 13:8–15 (pages 304–5), a report of what Saul did when the Philistine soldiers surrounding the Israelite army "were as many as the grains of sand on the seashore" (verse 5).

• When Samuel didn't show up soon enough, what did Saul choose to do?

> GOD ALLOWS BELIEVING MOMS TO HAVE TESTS— BUT IT'S ALWAYS AN OPEN-BOOK TEST.

• Why was this act wrong?

• What were the consequences of Saul's choosing to act rather than wait on the Lord?

• What does Saul's experience teach you and me about the value of waiting?

❧ This woman is nameless, she is not even a follower of God, and yet she still teaches us an important lesson. Turn to page 380 of *Mom's Bible* or 1 Kings 17:15 to meet the widow at Zarephath.

    • What steps of faith did the prophet Elijah ask this woman to take?

    • The widow had a choice: fear or trust. What fearful situation are you currently facing? What step(s) of faith does your circumstances call for? Have you asked God for courage to believe that He is working on your behalf?

    • What did the widow at Zarephath learn about God? And, according to the closing paragraph of her portrait, what lessons are available to us?

❧ Joseph faced a powerful temptation to commit the same sin that has ruined countless people and their families. Yet he chose to stay faithful to God even when no one was looking.

    • Read Genesis 39:7–9 (page 48)—and if it's hard to stop there, go ahead and read through verse 20. What reason did Joseph give for not having sexual relations with Potiphar's wife?

- What promise in 1 Corinthians 10:13 (page 1272) can help us make the right decision when we face temptation and no one is looking? This is a great verse to memorize with your kids.

❧ Becoming more like Jesus is God's ultimate purpose for each one of us who call Him Savior and Lord, so let's look at a few snapshots of Christ-like character from His life.

- In Matthew 4:1–10 (page 1029), what does Jesus show us about how to resist temptation?

- What do we learn about priorities in Matthew 14:23 (page 1047)?

- What example did Jesus set for us in John 13:1, 4, 5 (page 1179)?

What we truly believe about God is most clearly seen when it feels as though our world has fallen down around us—when we wonder if God is hearing our prayers—or if He will answer on time. Yet during those faith-refining times, our children are watching us and will learn important lessons about the unseen hand of God. The grace and trust with which we respond to difficult times will set a godly example for them.

Thank You, Lord God, for Your Word and what it teaches about trusting and staying faithful to You in hard times. Thank You for models like the widow at Zarephath, Joseph, and Jesus. Please give me the gift of faith to trust You as I do my best to lead my children to love You. Prepare them and strengthen their own faith for the future. Thank You for sustaining me in this season of waiting. Amen.

4. CHOOSE TO SUBMIT TO GOD'S WILL . . . HUMBLY

❧ Here are a few more snapshots from Jesus' life. In what ways did He submit to God's will?

- Matthew 24:36 (page 1063)
- Matthew 26:39, 42 (page 1067)
- Acts 1:6, 7 (page 1193)
- Philippians 2:6–8 (page 1312)

❧ Job was an honest and good man who pleased God and avoided evil, so Satan decided to test Job's faith—and God allowed it. What statement of faith—based on a big-picture and heavenly perspective—was Job able to make in Job 23:10 (page 549), despite the fact that he neither understood what God was doing nor consistently sensed His presence?

🕏 Turn to Isaiah 55:8 (page 784).

  • What is another reason why we are wise to submit to God's sovereign will?

  • Why is it good to serve a God we can know but not fully figure out?

> MOTHERHOOD IS GOD'S REFINING TOOL TO MAKE ME INTO THE WOMAN HE CREATED ME TO BE.

🕏 Now visit an amazing—and very familiar—thing that happened more than two thousand years ago in Nazareth. Read Luke 1:30–38 (page 1107). What do you appreciate and admire about Mary?

🕏 What current situation is inviting you—or forcing you—to submit to God's will? What is keeping you from submitting humbly? Ask God to help you follow in the steps of Job and Mary and Jesus.

> "Dying to self" often comes down to choosing whether or not to submit to God and His timing. We can make the choice to willingly surrender to His will when we take time to gaze upon God in all His glory and majesty. Join Mary as she humbly did this in Luke 1:46–55 (page 1108).

Lord, You wouldn't be a very big God if I could figure You out. Help me rest in the wonderful truth that You are an astounding and infinitely powerful, infinitely wise and loving God—especially when things are confusing and difficult for me to understand. Help me surrender my desires and rest in the promise of Your good plan for my life. Amen.

5. CHOOSE TO GIVE . . . GENEROUSLY

Read Exodus 35:4–9 (pages 108–9) and 36:4–7 (page 110). What do you find striking about the Israelites' example? What do you think prompted their generosity?

In 2 Corinthians 9:7 (page 1290), what does Paul teach us about our attitude when we give?

What does being able to give tithes and offerings—and to do so cheerfully—suggest about whom or what we are trusting? (Hint: 1 John 4:20, 21 [page 1392] and Matthew 7:9–11 [page 1034])

❧ At dinner tonight, go around the table and have each person share at least one memory of a time when your family was blessed by someone's cheerful generosity. Talk together about why you think these people were so kind.

❧ What can you and your family do together that would be cheerfully generous? Is there something you could do this weekend? Be prayerful and creative as you make your plans—and intentional in your conversation as you serve ("Isn't it fun to be able to share what God has given us?"; "We're able to be God's light when we share what He has given us"; "What can we do so our homebound neighbor [or the people at the nursing home or soup kitchen] know we're serving because we love Jesus?"; etc.).

When we are filled with His love, it's natural to notice someone who needs to receive a share in the bounty and mercy God's given to us. And we can enjoy giving it cheerfully.

Thank You, Lord, that You abundantly provide everything we need and more. May Your faithfulness and lavish grace prompt my own generosity—and please use me to grow in my children a generous heart attitude and the willingness to give joyfully. Amen.

LEAN ON ME: LEARNING FROM ONE ANOTHER

❧ Share one or two points from this week's study that were especially significant to you.

❧ What Scripture verse was especially meaningful when you came across it during your study? What instruction or encouragement did you receive from God's Spirit as you read that verse?

❧ God commands us to love with our actions, not just our words, and to serve with joy. What keeps us from loving and serving? How can we overcome the sin of self-absorption? Share ideas about serving amid the details of busy everyday life.

❧ Learn from one another by sharing answers to these questions:
  • What helps you stay faithful during life's difficult and dark days?
  • What helps you submit to God's will and His timing when you long to have things your way or when His will seems puzzling?

❧ What do you do to teach your kids about the following?
  • Serving joyfully?
  • Giving generously?

BRINGING IT HOME

The words Jesus spoke brought healing, hope, freedom, encouragement, and joy—and our words can do some of those very same things. What a good idea to give some word hugs to those who share our address.

Watch what happens, for instance, when Dad walks in and Mom and the kids shower him with word gifts like "Hooray! You're here!"; "I'm so glad you're home!"; and "I prayed for you today!"

Or your family can experience a blessing shower at the dinner table. Have each member of the family turn to the person on his or her left and say, "One of the things I love about you is . . ." Watch faces brighten in anticipation as each person gives and receives a word hug. This kind of dessert will be as satisfying for your heart as dinner was for your tummy!

LEAN ON HIM: LEARNING TO TRUST GOD

Ask every mom in the group to request prayer about one thing for herself or her nuclear family. Take notes so you'll be able to pray for your group members throughout the week.

Close by having someone pray the following:

Loving selflessly, serving joyfully, staying faithful, submitting to Your will, giving generously—Lord God, Your divine goal for us is to make us more like Jesus Christ. We thank You that You don't ask us to do this transforming work alone, but instead You have sent Your Spirit to transform us into Your Son's likeness. May we cooperate with the work Your Spirit wants to do in us so You will be glorified in all that we say, all that we do, and all that we are. Amen.

WALKING IN WISDOM: REVIEW AND REMEMBER

Choose to Love . . . Selflessly: Just as a picture is worth a thousand words, living out God's love with selfless actions speaks much more powerfully than a million words spoken about His grace and mercy.

Choose to Serve . . . Joyfully: Serving other people willingly and joyfully is a profound way to be God's light in this culture that lauds the wealthy, powerful, beautiful, athletic, and even the brazenly immoral.

Choose to Stay Faithful . . . Confidently: The better we know the truth about God, the easier we will find it to stay faithful during the times when He seems distant or quiet and during seasons of darkness and waiting.

Choose to Submit to God's Will . . . Humbly: Knowing well our heavenly Father—in all His goodness, power, love, wisdom, grace, and mercy—also helps us submit to His perfect will, just as Jesus and Mary, His mother, did.

Choose to Give . . . Generously: You show your trust in your faithful Provider, when you cheerfully and generously share what He has entrusted to you.

JUST FOR FUN

It's a basic and everyday miracle, so present in the world around us that we hardly even notice it. But you and your little ones are going to make time to notice and marvel.

Buy a package of lima bean seeds. Plant the seeds in several clear plastic cups. Discuss what plants need to grow. Daily check the plantings, and add water if the soil is dry.

In a few days you'll notice wondrous signs of life. Be amazed at the growth—and talk about how God celebrates as we mature spiritually. God loves us patiently as we grow—bit by bit, day by day—to be more like Jesus. And just as you are excited to see the lima bean begin to sprout, when God sees fruit in us, when He sees us being kind or patient just like Jesus would be, He is full of joy and delight.

YOU'VE GOT A FRIEND

You were called to be a mom. God has this specific assignment tailor-made for you. It has your name on it. Your vocation is holy. Your family is God's gift to you, and with it comes a whole new set of spiritual, mental, emotional, and physical challenges. But because of God's gracious provision, you don't ever need to walk this road alone. Instead, you can thankfully welcome the support God has for you—His Word, His presence, your spouse and family, fellow moms, friends, and your church family.

MOM TIME

1. GOD

⁂ What reassuring truth does the second part of Psalm 139:16 (page 651) proclaim? When and why might that be especially comforting for moms?

⁂ Read Nehemiah 8:10 (page 510), and focus on the last clause. What source of strength does God provide us? What reasons do Christ-following moms have for being joyful?

❧ What amazing and wonderful promise does Jesus speak of in the second part of Matthew 28:20 (page 1072)? Reflect on a mommy moment when you especially sensed Jesus' presence with you.

❧ When have you experienced the truth of 2 Corinthians 12:9 (page 1292) specifically in the realm of parenting?

❧ What exhortation in 1 Thessalonians 5:17 (page 1329) is wise parenting advice?

It's no surprise that the Word of God—from the One who created our children and has entrusted them to our care—offers hope and guidance for us as we raise our children to know Him, love Him, and serve Him.

Your sovereign plan, Your strength, Your constant presence with me, Your strength filling me when I am weak, the power of prayer—Lord God, You are my perfect Provider. Thank You for giving me everything I need to parent the children You've blessed me with. I believe Your promises; help my unbelief! Amen.

2. DAD, GRANDPARENTS, AND SIBLINGS

❧ Your husband is God's gift to you—your best friend, companion, and teammate in parenting. As the father of your children, he is an invaluable gift to them. What can you do sometime this week to show your husband that you appreciate him?

❧ Do you treat your husband with the same kindness that you would treat a friend? What did friends do for each of these characters—Moses and the lame man—in these passages?

• Exodus 17:10–13 (page 88)

• Mark 2:1–5 (page 1075)

> IF YOU SEE A BIBLE FALLING APART, IT USUALLY BELONGS TO SOMEONE WHO ISN'T.

❧ In what ways has your husband done one or both of these things for you? Have you specifically recognized his help? Can you speak words of appreciation or admiration to him like "Thank you!" or "You amaze me!" when he helps you in any way this week? Let him know you need his support and are grateful for it.

❧ Turn to the "Wonderful Counselor" feature on page 7 of *Mom's Bible.* Consider which of the six ideas might be a good one to implement first in your marriage—and do so prayerfully and expectantly. God wants your marriage to display His glory.

❧ Ephesians 6:1–4 (page 1308) offers some guidelines for parents. (By the way, Ephesians 6:1 is one of the first verses you'll want your kids to memorize.)

- What does this passage suggest about the importance of you and your husband being in agreement on the rules and the consequences you establish for your kids?

- What does this passage imply about the importance of a husband's involvement in raising your kids? Are you allowing him to lead and giving him opportunity to be a teacher, or are you demanding more control or demeaning his suggestions? Be honest. Your husband is not perfect, but you are called to be his teammate, living in mutual agreement with him as you parent together (Ephesians 5:21, page 1307).

❧ Although we establish our own family rules and traditions, our parents, in-laws, and other relatives can enrich our family and provide valuable assistance.

- In what ways have your parents or your husband's parents been helpful? How often do you let them know you appreciate their support?

- What issues or concerns about grandparent involvement—or lack of involvement—do you have? Are you praying and asking for Christlike reactions and attitudes? You can pray to be a peacemaker, assuming the best of your parents, even if they do things in a different way than you would choose. Remembering that "different does not mean defective" can help you choose to be gentle, not judgmental.

- What benefits come when loving, praying grandparents are involved in a grandchild's life?

⁂ When God blessed you with your children, He also gave them to one another. Do you encourage your children to treat one another with kindness? And are you careful to give love freely to each child and not compare one to another? What statements will encourage bonding between your kids when you see rivalry or bickering? ("What you just said to your brother sounded disrespectful. Your brother is your best friend. Let's try that again, and speak to him like you're talking to your friend.") How can you encourage mutual celebration so that they'll be friends when they grow up?

Lord, raising a child is not a one-person or even a single-generation job. Please help me to wholeheartedly embrace my husband's partnership, to warmly and wisely welcome grandparents, and to playfully, but firmly encourage the siblings to also become each other's best friends. Thank You for the foundation of a solid support system that You have provided in my husband, our parents, and our kids. Amen.

---

3. THE SISTERHOOD OF MOMS

❧ Consider some pairs of friends who have been immortalized in Scripture.

- **Jonathan and David:** Describe the friendship found in 1 Samuel 20 or in the notes found on page 315 of *Mom's Bible*. Do you have a Jonathan in your life? Are you a Jonathan for someone else? Ask God to provide such a friendship for you—a godly woman who loves you, wants God's best for you, and prays for your children. Also ask God to allow you the privilege of being that kind of "sister" for a special girlfriend.

- **Elijah and Elisha:** Now turn to page 391 of *Mom's Bible* or 2 Kings 2 to meet another pair of friends. What do you appreciate about Elijah and Elisha's friendship? Does the description remind you of any of your own friendships? Thank God for the gift of your soul-sister or ask Him to provide one for you. Pray specifically for the Lord Jesus to provide each of your children with such a healthy Christian friendship.

- **Paul and Barnabas:** On page 1219 of *Mom's Bible*, you'll get a snapshot of another special partnership found in Acts 15. What do you find significant about the relationship between Paul and Barnabas? Who is a Barnabas (his name means "Son of Encouragement") in your life? And for whom are you a Barnabas?

❧ Now let's peek in on a woman-to-woman friendship, that of **Mary and Elizabeth**. Read Luke 1:39–45 and, also, the "Walking in Friendship" section on page 1108 of *Mom's Bible*.

• What reason for rejoicing did the two women share?

• Think back on your first pregnancy or adoption. What did you appreciate about being with other pregnant women or adoptive mothers during that season? How wonderful that God provided the older Elizabeth and the young, unmarried Mary with each other!

❧ The sisterhood of moms is key to our parenting efforts, and it is wonderful when we have deep relationships with moms who are at our own stage of the mothering journey—as well as godly moms who have already experienced the same challenges and joys we have. Think about those moms who have blessed you, moms who offer their support as a sounding board, counselor, mentor, and fellow struggler. Describe a time when you experienced support from "sisters" that has been vital on your mothering journey.

Can you think of a woman "behind" you on your journey that would be blessed by your experience? Whatever your age or stage, you have experience as a mom that can be a support to younger women or children. What kids are you praying for or encouraging in faith? You may be the only woman who is praying for someone who needs God's touch right now. Ask Jesus for a name. Your experience and willingness to pray make you an invaluable resource to newer moms, especially those who don't have family nearby or anyone who prays for them.

> Speaking of those who have blessed us, when I was eight years old, a mom in my neighborhood prayed for me, invited me into her home, told me about Jesus, and took me to church. Every person in my family was transformed and became a believer by the time I was ten, all because a neighbor cared about our souls, prayed for us, and loved us in practical ways. How eternally grateful I am for our neighborhood angel . . . a gift from Jesus.

Lord God, thank You for other moms You have put in my life to encourage and pray for me, to teach and inspire me. Because I am thankful for mentors who have shaped me, I want to pass on the blessing. Open my eyes and heart to a mom You want me to come alongside in Your name and with Your love. Amen.

4. BUILDING FRIENDSHIPS IN CHRIST

❧ As moms, we have many circles of friends—moms from our kids' school and sports teams, moms we meet at the gym, moms we carpool with, moms from church. Some are acquaintances, and many are friends. But the Bible gives specific guidelines for our closest friends in Proverbs 27:17 (page 690).

- Sparks can fly when iron strikes iron. But, metaphorically speaking, what good can result when sparks fly between Christian friends?

- Describe how Christian moms you know are "sharpening" you.

❧ Every good gift comes from our heavenly Father (James 1:17, page 1367), and godly friends are among God's most precious gifts. But we have the choice of whether or not to receive those gifts.

- What mom do you think God might be trying to use in your heart and life as a "gift"? Can you ask God to soften your heart so you're ready to receive His provision?

❧ Read Psalm 1 (page 566). How does it affect you when you spend time with someone who constantly displays a critical spirit, cynical tongue, or gossiping lips? Do you laugh at jokes that deride husbands? Or stay in the presence of those who stir up dissention? What can you do to avoid the temptation of toxic people in your circle of friends?

❧ There is a saying, "Show me your friends and I'll show you yourself." When we choose our friends, it is important that we choose people who will build us up in faith or, to use Paul's words, who "help others become stronger" (Ephesians 5:29, page 1308). And this is true and even crucial advice for our kids as well! What are you doing—or could you be doing—to encourage your kids to choose friends wisely?

❧ God's Word provides discernment for choosing good friends. Read Ecclesiastes 4:9–12 (page 700). List some blessings that come with well-chosen friends.

❧ What warning do you find in 2 Corinthians 6:14 (page 1288)? Can you think of a way to illustrate that truth for your kids? (Oil and water come to mind, but you may have a more creative option for your children.)

❧ Turn to John 15:15 (page 1183). What does it mean to you that Jesus calls you "friend"? John 15:13 is one answer (praise God!), but what discernment do you receive and what difference can it make in your day-to-day parenting that Jesus calls you "friend"?

Godly friends are a blessing beyond measure. Proverbs 27:6 (page 689) says, "The slap of a friend can be trusted to help you." There are times when you and I need to be challenged, and that's when a godly friend's admonition may keep us from going in the wrong direction.

Thank You, Lord, for friends who point me to You, who keep me on Your path, who rejoice when I rejoice and mourn when I mourn, and who pray and believe Your best for me when, during life's tough times, I am unable to pray and believe. And, Lord, help me to be Your friend so I can become a wise and good friend to others. Amen.

5. YOUR CHURCH FAMILY

Most of what your children learn about the Lord's love and about the joy of being part of His church family will be caught from you, not taught by you. How contagious is your love for God's family? Your answers to these questions may help you identify areas that need help.

- We'll start with a basic issue: How faithfully do you attend the weekend worship service?

- What personal involvement in church programs and activities do your children see?

• What kind of financial giving—and what kind of attitude toward that giving—do your kids observe?

• How often do your children hear you express or even demonstrate your genuine appreciation for your pastor, church, and for church leaders?

• Which staff members and which aspects of the church's life and ministry does your family pray for regularly?

❧ Please turn to the "Walking in Commitment" section on page 452 of *Mom's Bible* (1 Chronicles 28:10) for some important truths about the church. What do you find that encourages or challenges you to be actively involved in a local church body?

❧ The early church in Acts sets a wonderful example for believers today. Read Acts 2:44–47 (page 1198).

• What characterized this early fellowship?

• Which of these activities and blessings have you experienced?

• Read the "Walking in Fellowship" feature on page 1198 of *Mom's Bible* (Acts 2:44). What benefits of being involved in a church do our kids experience?

❧ Inviting our church family to come alongside us as we raise our kids is a wise and important step.

   • Read 1 Samuel 1:24–28 (pages 291–92). What did Hannah do here, and why?

   • What are some reasons we dedicate our children today?

> CHURCH IS A PLACE OF POSSIBILITIES . . . OF MARRIAGES THAT DO LAST FOR A LIFETIME, OF MEN AND WOMEN WHO DO FINISH WELL, OF CHILDREN WHO ARE BEING NURTURED IN THE FAITH, AND OF FAMILIES THAT DO PRAY TOGETHER. MIRACLES HAPPEN AT CHURCH. DON'T MISS IT!

• If you have attended a baby dedication, what kind of support does the church family pledge to the child's parents? Why is that pledge an important gift to the child and his/her family?

In the church we experience God's love in a tangible way unequaled anywhere else. His people become the hands and feet and heart of Jesus for us. In fact, His people are the family we don't have by blood. When Jesus instructed us to pray saying, "Our Father," He was telling us who our brothers and sisters are. His plan is for us to experience His church—His amazing grace through His people.

As moms—as Christian moms in a dark world—we need help raising our kids. Thankfully, God provides that help through a variety of relationships. Our husbands, parents, and kids; other moms; friends; our church family—God uses all of these people to support us in our efforts to raise our kids to honor and glorify Him. Don't miss out on these powerful, even life-changing, relationships!

Lord, thank You that You call us and our children into Your body of believers—the local church—to learn more about You and Your love, to experience a kind of community the world can't offer, and to be encouraged and strengthened to be Your people. I want my family to receive the blessings You have for us in the church—and we want You to use us to bless our brothers and sisters in Your family. Amen.

LEAN ON ME: LEARNING FROM ONE ANOTHER

❧ Share one or two points from this week's study that were especially significant to you.

❧ What Scripture verse was especially meaningful when you came across it during your study? What instruction or encouragement did you receive from God's Spirit as you read that verse?

❧ In what specific ways have you experienced God's presence and His provision for you on your parenting journey? It is helpful to make talk of God's provision and references to Jesus' constant presence with us a standard part of family conversation. You might say, for example, "Lord, we pray for Abby as she goes to this birthday party. Help her to think about how others feel and include everyone" or "Thank You, Lord, for protecting Luke when he was climbing that tree." Look for opportunities to naturally celebrate God's faithfulness in simple ways with your children at home. List some possibilities here.

❧ Talk together about some of the challenges and blessings of Dad's involvement in raising kids, of grandparents' involvement, and of siblings. Get tips from each other on topics such as letting go of your controlling way of doing things so Dad feels confident in his role as father, setting healthy boundaries with grandparents, and minimizing rivalry between siblings.

❧ Once again, take advantage of this time to learn from one another. Discuss this question from your individual study and learn from one another's answers: *What are you doing—or could you be doing—to encourage your kids to choose friends wisely?*

BRINGING IT HOME

Who has encouraged you on your faith journey? All of us need one another in the body of Christ!

As you've journeyed through life, who has influenced you, mentored you, accepted you, forgiven you, admonished you, and/or prayed for you? God may have blessed you with several people who have helped you at different times on your faith journey, at every stage of your life. Have you said thank you?

Choose one person to thank this week and one the following week. Send a note or contact those people to say how much they mean to you. Tell them what you admire about them and how God used them in your life. If one such person is already with Jesus in heaven, you can honor that person by passing on to someone else a similar kind of encouragement that this special friend gave you.

LEAN ON HIM: LEARNING TO TRUST GOD

Ask every mom in the group to request prayer about one thing for herself or her nuclear family. Take notes so you'll be able to pray for your group members throughout the week.

Close by having someone pray the following:

Lord God, Creator of families, help us to honor You by making You the most important part of our family's life. As we build our family, we will talk together about You—about Your faithfulness, Your greatness, Your commands, and Your blessings. Help us to creatively make faith in You as normal as going to work or the grocery store and as natural as commenting on the weather. Give to all of us, Lord Jesus, hearts of adoration. We want to obey Your commandments and include You in everything we do, because we love You with all our hearts. Amen.

WALKING IN WISDOM: REVIEW AND REMEMBER

God: The Almighty planned for us to have the kids we have; His Word is our instruction manual, His joy can be our source of strength as we parent; Jesus is with us always; His strength is made perfect in our weakness; and He gives us the privilege of prayer so that we can talk over every detail of our journey with the One who called us to be moms.

Dad, Grandparents, and Siblings: With their wisdom, prayer, help, and warmth, we benefit from the support encircling our family. Everyone functions best—our kids, Dad, and grandparents—when we don't try to do this parenting thing alone.

The Sisterhood of Moms: Moms have lots to offer one another, whether our kids are the same ages or we're all at different stages of the journey. Ask God to give you some noble mom friends—and ask Him to help you select someone who needs you to be her godly mentoring friend.

Building Friendships in Christ: God can and will guide our choice of friends and our kids' choices as well, for He knows how important godly companions and kindred spirits are for our journey through this world.

Your Church Family: When we join with fellow believers to hear from God and His Word every week, to learn more about Jesus, to share His love, to be with people living out the same priorities, and to celebrate His goodness, we benefit—and so do our kids. We are wise to make involvement in God's life-changing, lifesaving community a focal point for our families.

✂❧ JUST FOR FUN ❧✄

Get outside with your kids and play—whatever their ages, whatever the season. If the leaves are on the ground, experience the joy of crunching and shuffling through them. If the dandelions are puffy, share the fun of blowing those feathery seeds off the stem. Take a rain walk, complete with boots and umbrellas—and stomp in every puddle you see. Or, on a warm day, tackle washing the car together, "accidentally" squirting one another with the hose . . . and then all of you (yes, you, Mom!) run through the sprinklers. If you want to capture the memories, get your camera ready and let your kids take a mud bath!

7

LAUNCHING OUR KIDS TOWARD THEIR GOD-GIVEN DREAMS

"What do you want to be when you grow up?"

Children will undoubtedly have a variety of answers through the years.

Maybe your daughter aspires to be a bareback rider in a circus when she is five . . . then she dreams of being a professional soccer star . . . and, later, an elementary school teacher.

Maybe our young son first wants to be a truck driver . . . then he decides firefighting might be his thing . . . and, later, high school teacher, then engineer . . .

As moms, along with our husbands, we are privileged to help our children explore their interests, pursue their passions, and develop their talents. We also pray for them and guide them so they move toward precisely what the Lord has gifted them for and has called them to be. We help them identify their dreams according to God's leading, and we do what we can to help fuel those God-given desires and dreams until they become reality. We teach our children, day by day, to live their life for an audience of One even as we strive to do the same.

MOM TIME

1. GROWING UP

❧ It is an amazing privilege and blessing to be a mom. Consider, for instance, all that the Lord teaches us through our kids. What is one lesson He's taught you about His love, patience, or forgiveness since you've become a mother?

❧ What does Psalm 139:13–16 (page 651) say about your child? What hope and peace do you find in those verses?

❧ The thought is mind-boggling, but Jesus Himself was a crying infant, a teething baby, a curious toddler, and a teenager who outgrew his tunic. What do we learn about His growth in Luke 2:40 (page 1111)?

❧ What role do you think Mary and Joseph played in that growth (see Luke 2:52)?

❧ What dreams do you remember having as a child? Ask your husband the same thing. Are you listening to what your child says about his/her passions, and are you willing to allow your child to explore in areas that are not your own passion? What are you currently doing to help your children follow their inclination or bent as they grow?

The most important thing I want for my children is for them to be holy. Happiness will follow if their hearts are right.

Lord Jesus, You have crafted my children in amazing and wonderful ways. Thank You for sharing these precious people with me. I'm asking You to guide my children so that they become strong spiritually and physically, wise in their knowledge of You, blessed by Your favor and goodness, and able to follow the dreams You give them. Amen.

2. KNOWING YOUR CHILDREN

❧ What does Psalm 127:3 (page 645) say about children?

❧ Since our children are gifts from God, we are to be good stewards of each one of them just as we are stewards of all God's other gifts to us. Our first and greatest responsibility is to evangelize and disciple our children. As Christian moms, you and I have the privilege of leading them to know Jesus for their own salvation, and then encouraging them to follow the Holy Spirit and the desires of their hearts that God gives them. If that's a new thought, what is your reaction?

❧ The heart of the issue is the heart. What character or personality traits (such as leadership, compassion, or sensitivity to God's voice) does each of your children display? Have you affirmed this trait as a unique gift? What does—or could—your encouragement look like for each child?

❧ I'd like you to meet Samson's mom. Read Judges 13:4, 5 and, if you want, "Samson's Mother Entertains an Angel" on page 272 of *Mom's Bible*. What specific instructions did God's messenger give Samson's mom so that Samson could become the person God wanted him to be? In what ways do we protect or guard our children so that they are "set apart" for God's purposes? What things in the culture must we say no to at various times? Can you think of a time when it was difficult for you or your children to be "different"?

❧ In order for you to determine the plans God has for your child, be a student of your child. What God-given talents, interests, and/or passions have you noticed? What does—or could—your stewardship of those talents, interests, and passions look like? Consider books, possible mentors, and real-life opportunities—and encourage your kids each step of the way.

> Be a student of your children so that you can use every means to influence your child's heart to love Christ and be an effective discipler of their talents, interests, and personality traits as well as a confident encourager of their God-given dreams.

Lord, it is an amazing privilege to be appointed by You to be a steward of my children. Thank You—and thank You that You don't make that appointment and then disappear. Instead, You are equipping and encouraging me every day. Please give me wisdom to support each of them as they develop their talents, pursue the dreams You give them, and serve Your people according to the ways You have gifted them. And may all they do bring You glory. Amen.

3. Sensing God's Direction

❧ It is an easily misunderstood verse, but its actual message offers much hope and reassurance to moms.

• What promise does God make in Psalm 37:4 (page 588)?

• God plants in our hearts the desires that will please Him, and then He helps us fulfill those desires (Philippians 2:13, page 1312). In that sense, He will give you the desires of your heart. Share an example from your own life.

> ASK GOD WHAT HE HAS IN MIND FOR YOUR CHILD. HE WILL INSTRUCT YOU AND TEACH YOU SO YOUR CHILD WILL BE PREPARED FOR THE FUTURE.

• As a mom, what are a few things you can do to help your child be receptive to the desires God has for him/her?

❧ Now look at Jeremiah 29:11 (pages 834–35). What promise do you find there?

❧ The apostle Paul knew the importance of being attuned to what God wants for us and to live in a way that pleases Him, our audience of One. What did Paul proclaim in these two passages?

- 1 Corinthians 4:3, 4b (page 1266)

- Acts 24:16 (page 1233)

❧ What helps you personally keep focused on your audience of One?

❧ What can you do to adapt those things for your children, whatever their ages?

God will guide our children by putting His desires for them in their hearts. We must be willing to let them follow those desires in fulfillment of His good plans for them. As teenagers, this could mean a short-term mission trip. When they grow up, this could mean a call to service in another part of the country or world. Following God's plan is not about our children staying near our homes. Instead, our prayer should be that our kids hunger for a closeness to God so they may live out His good plans for them . . . for their own delight and the Father's glory.

Lord, we live in a world that says, "Follow your heart" and "Do your own thing"; a noisy world that tries to dictate right and wrong; and a confusing world where we can't please everyone. Please, Lord, guard my children's hearts and help them grow up wanting to follow Your ways, making decisions according to Your standards, and seeking to please You and You alone. Amen.

4. SHARING YOUR FAITH

❧ What command do we find in Matthew 28:19, 20 (page 1072)?

❧ A mom's fulfillment of this Great Commission to make disciples of all nations starts with her family. Let's first make sure that we have our message straight. What key qualities of the gospel message do you find in the following verses?

- Romans 3:23 (page 1243)
- Romans 6:23 (page 1247)

- 2 Corinthians 5:21 (page 1287)

- Ephesians 2:8 (page 1302)

- Romans 10:9 (page 1253)

❧ Now look at the instructions to parents found in Deuteronomy 6:4–9 (page 199). What could obedience to verses 7–9 look like in your home today?

❧ Bedtime stories can have eternal significance. Tonight, tell your own salvation story or about a time when God showed you His goodness or His faithfulness or His love. Build up the suspense. Celebrate who God is. Remind your children that He is the same yesterday, today, and forever and that they can count on Him. And tell them that they can share stories of God's goodness as well, especially as they grow and look for God's special care. One more thought: You just may want to keep a journal of their stories.

It's an amazing privilege—introducing your kids to their heavenly Father, teaching them the gospel, and learning from them what it is to have childlike faith.

Lord, what an honor to teach my children the glorious truth about who You are, how much You love them, and about Jesus' death and resurrection for their salvation. Help me be clear, consistent, and joyful in my teaching. And, by Your Spirit, please work in their hearts so that one day they are walking with You—and will continue to love You all their days. Amen.

5. LETTING GO

❧ Successful Christian parenting has been wisely and accurately defined as transferring our children's dependence on us to their dependence on the Lord Jesus. According to these passages, to what kind of heavenly Father are we introducing our children?

• Psalm 100:1–5 (page 626)

• Isaiah 40:12–14 (page 762)

• Jeremiah 10:6, 7 (page 812)

❧ What promise do you find in Proverbs 22:6 (page 682)?

❧ What instruction does Proverbs 22:15 (page 683) imply?

> YOU CAN'T PARENT FROM THE BACK OF YOUR HEAD. WHAT DO YOU NEED TO TURN OFF OR SHUT DOWN IN ORDER TO SPEND FACE-TO-FACE TIME WITH YOUR CHILD?

❧ It's a single verse—and a huge act of faith. Read Exodus 2:1–4 (page 65). The *she* is Jochebed; the *he*, baby Moses. Now read through verse 10. We have a wonderful mentor in Jochebed: she loved Moses enough to let him go, and she trusted his safety to God's care.

  • On what "river" are you about to release your children?

  • What have you done/are you doing to prepare them?

  • What evidence of God's sovereignty did Jochebed experience (verses 8, 9)? Is that an encouragement to you?

❧ What fears for your children do you need to place into God's capable hands? He can supply the faith to believe His goodness, to replace the fear that freezes you. Ask Him for the gift of faith, and then write out 1 John 4:18 (page 1392) as a reminder of both God's great love for you and His greater-love-than-yours for your children.

God knows our tomorrows better than we know our yesterdays. He knows the good and gracious path He has chosen for our children. We can release them into His care because God's grace will be enough.

As moms, you and I are called to be—like Jochebed—faithful caretakers of our children while they are in our homes. Day by day we prepare our children to serve God by teaching them His truth and disciplining them in His ways. We help our children learn to both listen to God and pursue His plans for them. We encourage our kids to pursue those God-given desires, and we pray for them each step of the way. We seal their boats, inside and out, with God's Word and our prayers. Then we launch them, trusting our sovereign God to protect and care for them, wherever the river takes them.

Lord Jesus, there will come a day when I will release to You these precious children You have entrusted to me. I'm glad that You will always be with them; I pray that they will always choose to walk with You. In the meantime, Lord, help me be the mom my children need, the mom You want me to be to them. I need Your wisdom, Your strength, and Your guidance—and I'm so glad You can redeem my efforts. Amen.

LEAN ON ME: LEARNING FROM ONE ANOTHER

❧ Share one or two points from this week's study that were especially significant to you.

❧ What Scripture verse was especially meaningful when you came across it during your study? What instruction or encouragement did you receive from God's Spirit as you read that verse?

❧ We are stewards of the children God entrusts to our care; our kids actually belong to Him, their heavenly Father. In what ways do you find this truth convicting? In what ways do you find it freeing?

❧ What do you find most challenging about passing your love for Jesus on to your children? What resources are most helpful as you try to meet this challenge?

❧ Which of God's unchanging characteristics make it easier for you to think about one day letting go of your children? Share why as you praise Him.

BRINGING IT HOME

Jesus calls us to become like little children in order to experience the kingdom of God. So this week, let the little girl inside of you take some time to play. What is something that you loved to do as a girl and still enjoy? Is it dabbling in art, playing music, exploring nature, exercising, reading, creating . . . or something else?

Now, keeping in mind the five senses, plan something that excites you and appeals to sight, sound, touch, taste, and/or smell . . . Browse through an art exhibit, gift store, or antique shop . . . visit a bookstore . . . attend a concert or a play . . . take a cooking class . . . walk barefoot on the beach. Whatever it is, spend some slow moments doing something that brings you joy. Refreshing yourself like this will rekindle the little-girl passion for life that fuels your endurance for mundane tasks and energizes you for the hard work of parenting.

Know that the God who loves kids also loves to see your childlike delight in His world.

LEAN ON HIM: LEARNING TO TRUST GOD

Ask every mom in the group to request prayer for one thing for herself or her nuclear family. Go around the circle and ask, "How can we pray for you this week?" Take notes so you'll be able to pray for your group members throughout the week.

Close by having someone pray the following:

Father in heaven, it is truly amazing to think that You have entrusted Your precious children to our care. Thank You for being with us each challenging step of the way and for helping us to launch them into Your divine purpose. Keep us seeking Your wisdom, peace, and strength. Keep us mindful that You love our children more than we do and that Your plans for them are always good. Again, thank You that we are privileged

to be part of Your plans for our children. Help us be faithful and effective stewards and trust You with our fears. We ask this in Jesus' name and for Your glory. Amen.

WALKING IN WISDOM: REVIEW AND REMEMBER

Growing Up: Your kids teach you about God's love for you even as you teach them about His great love for them, and those lessons foster spiritual growth and strength in both generations.

Knowing Your Children: As you pay attention to your children's interests, talents, passions, and character traits, God will show you how to nurture and grow those for your kids' good and His glory.

Sensing God's Direction: God plants seeds of His good plans for them in your children's hearts, and you have the privilege and responsibility of helping them live out those plans for their good and His glory.

Sharing Your Faith: Teaching your kids the gospel, living out God's mercy and grace, telling them stories of His faithfulness—what an honor and a privilege! And God Himself will help you.

Letting Go: Ideally, the end result of your parenting will be children who are successfully launched to pursue and fulfill their God-given dreams—and more dependent on the Lord than on you. But that won't keep you from wanting and needing to pray for them as they travel down the river of life. Your heart will be with them at every turn.

JUST FOR FUN

❧ Together with your children, read Exodus 16:4–16 (page 85), and talk about how amazing and faithful God is.

- How often did God give His people manna?

- How long would the manna usually last?

- When would the manna last longer?

- Why did He want His people to come for manna six days a week instead of once a week or once a month? He could have made the manna last that long. (By the way, did you know that manna means "what is it?"?)

- Jesus is our Bread of Life, and He wants us—and our kids—to come to Him each and every day with our needs and concerns. Whether it is while sitting at the breakfast table or nestled on the sofa, as often as you can in the course of the week, gather with your kids, read together from God's Word, and talk about how amazing and faithful He is.